STRANGE BUT TRUE
NORTH CAROLINA

SWEETWATER
PRESS

Strange But True North Carolina

Copyright © 2007 Cliff Road Books, Inc.

Produced by arrangement with Sweetwater Press

ISBN-13: 978-1-58173-521-5
ISBN-10: 1-58173-521-9

Design by Miles G. Parsons
Map of North Carolina by Tim Rocks

Printed in The United States of America

STRANGE BUT TRUE
NORTH CAROLINA

Lynne L. Hall

SWEETWATER
PRESS

TABLE OF CONTENTS

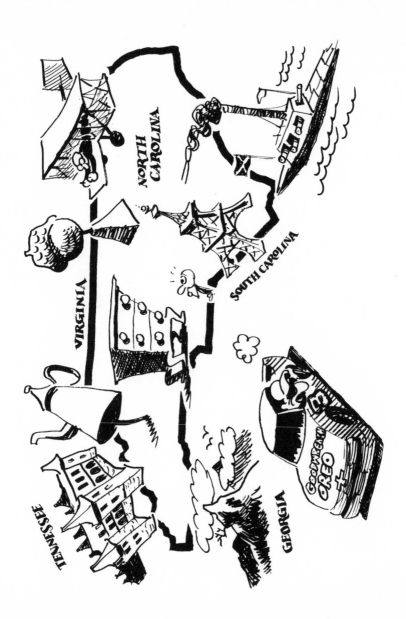

In a Strange State:

Road Trip Through Strange But True North Carolina

Do you know the state you're in? What we mean is, do you really know North Carolina? The state tourism department wants you to learn all about their state. Discover the state you're in, they say, and you'll see rolling rivers, charming small towns, and bustling cities. Read their brochures, watch their slick television commercials, and you'll be regaled by the many scenic beauties of the Old North State. And, no doubt about it, there are plenty to see.

Along North Carolina's western edge, the Appalachian Mountain range forms a lush forest landscape. The Great Smoky Mountains in the southwest are one of the country's most popular—and beautiful—destinations. A 250-mile stretch of the Blue Ridge Parkway winds through North Carolina's mountains, culminating in Mount Mitchell, the highest peak in the eastern United States.

Covered with more than one hundred twenty different varieties of hardwoods, the entire mountain range blazes with a riot of colors in the fall. And, although North Carolina is the quintessential Southern state, with areas of magnolia-shaded indolence, there also are areas that see thirty inches of snow annually. Here, summers are cool with low humidity.

In a Strange State

In the center of the state lie the gently rolling foothills of the Piedmont region. This area holds the largest cities and the biggest financial institutions. Here, renowned research universities, textile and furniture factories, and shopping meccas abut historic landmarks and tobacco farms.

North Carolina's eastern edge runs into the deep blue waters of the Atlantic Ocean, forming pristine beaches and wetlands teeming with wildlife. The Outer Banks, a chain of fragile barrier islands, are the defining characteristic of this area. Beautiful, historic homes and lighthouses dot this area, encompassing more than a hundred miles of unspoiled coastline and surrounded by nine hundred square miles of water.

Ahh, but there's another North Carolina lurking behind all that beauty and elegance, and it's a state of pure wackiness—a state filled with eccentric characters, crazy happenings, extraordinary, weird, sometimes even spooky, places, and some of the most bizarre landmarks ever built. So drop that colorful tourism brochure. Turn off the pretty commercials. Come tour our Strange But True North Carolina. You'll be glad you discovered it!

Forget purple mountain majesties and coastal beauty, we've got Blowing Rock and Barney the Bear. There's the Land of Oz, the World's Largest Ten Commandments, giant furniture, and a whole slew of weirded out museums. And, oh! Don't miss the trip out to Mayberry, where Andy and Opie live in perpetuity.

So make sure the chariot's in good working order and let's hit those back roads. Really strange wonders await you!

Strange Statues

We've Got Statues

Scattered willy-nilly across Strange But True North Carolina is an eclectic collection of strange and quirky monuments. You'll find a whole crew of Muffler Men, giant pigs, and, oh my, a decidedly risque set of concrete gams.

ACORN • RALEIGH

Holy Smokes! It's enough to give a flying squirrel a snack attack! Rocky might break his teeth on this snack, however, for Raleigh's giant acorn is made of copper. The 1,250-pound acorn was designed by artist David Benson for Raleigh's bicentennial. Why an acorn? Of course there's a good reason. You see, Raleigh is known as the City of Oaks for all the beautiful oak trees lining its streets.

Raleigh's Acorn weighs 1,250 pounds.
Photo by Renee Wright.

Strange Statues

Those folks in Raleigh really know how to party, too. In their "First Night Raleigh" New Year's Eve celebration, they run the big nut up a pole and drop it one hundred feet at midnight. Happy New Year!

Located in Moore Square at the corner of Blount and Martin streets.

ANDY AND OPIE • MOUNT AIRY/RALEIGH

Do you miss Mayberry? If something about that wonderful small Southern town rings true, there's good reason. Andy Griffith, who created Mayberry and played Sheriff Andy Taylor in the 1960s television hit, *The Andy Griffith Show*, was born and raised in good ol' Mount Airy, North Carolina. He based Mayberry and, no doubt, many of its denizens, on his hometown and his experiences growing up there.

The show got its start as an episode of the popular show *The Danny Thomas Show* in 1960, in which Danny Thomas's character is arrested in Mayberry for running a stop sign—at a crossroad that has yet to be built. The arresting officer, of course, is Sheriff Andy Taylor and throughout the episode a steady stream of Mayberry characters parades through with a variety of comedic antics. The episode was so well received that it was spun off into *The Andy Griffith Show* that same year.

One night a week for the next eight years, America dropped in on Sheriff Taylor in Mayberry, where there was no need to lock your doors and a crime wave meant the local moonshiners had produced a bumper crop. For that short time, we became neighbors to Andy, Opie, Aunt Bee, and Barney. We snickered at the antics of Gomer and Goober. Giggled when Otis, the town drunk, locked himself into his jail cell on Saturday nights. Howled at the "It's me! It's me! It's Ernest T.!" greeting of Ernest T. Bass.

Today, Mayberry and its citizens live in syndication, still making us homesick for a time and place that never really existed. Those wishing to pay homage, though, can visit Mount Airy, where bronze statues of Andy and Opie hold a place of honor. Located on the front lawn of the Andy Griffith Playhouse, the statues depict the scene of the show's opening, with Andy and Opie, fishing poles over their shoulders, moseying down to the local fishing hole.

A plaque honoring "A sweeter time, a gentler place," was set in concrete at the base of the statue. Unfortunately, a crime wave of Mayberry portions hit Mount Airy and the plaque was stolen six months after dedication of the statues.

The Mount Airy tableau is a replica of the one first dedicated in Raleigh. Those original statues, dedicated by the TV Land television network, were created by Studio EIS of New York. They're installed in Pullen Park in Raleigh, a town often mentioned in Mayberry as the "big city."

Located at 218 Rockford Street, Mount Airy, and 520 Ashe Avenue, Raleigh.

BASEBALL WATER TOWER • ZEBULON

If you're a big baseball fan, and we do mean BIG, then you should take a trip to Zebulon, where there's a really big baseball. It's actually a water tower standing outside Five County Stadium, home of the Carolina Mudcats, North Carolina's minor league baseball team.

Located at 1501 State Highway 39.

BICYCLE • HIGH POINT

The Jolly Green Giant has lost his ride. It's sitting on top of a building—a bike shop, no doubt—in High Point.

Located on Route 311.

BIG CHAIR • THOMASVILLE

Home of the Thomasville Chair Company (now known as Thomasville Furniture Industries), Thomasville had become known as the "Chair City" by 1922. That year, someone, probably a PR guy, hatched the idea to build a giant chair to promote the town's biggest industry.

The chair, a simple straight-backed chair, was built by the Thomasville Chair company, using enough lumber to build a hundred such chairs. When completed, it stood twenty-three feet, six inches tall, and was covered in leather made from the hide of a Swiss steer.

For more than fifteen years, the chair served as a fitting attraction for the town. Alas, exposure to the harsh elements took its toll and the chair was finally scrapped. In 1948, the Chamber of Commerce decided to build a chair that would last forever—or at least until the next millennium.

Chamber of Commerce Manager Kenneth Hoyle approached James Buford Harvey, a local artist who had built the town's life-sized concrete lion, and asked him if he could build a concrete chair—a really, really big concrete chair. Always one up for a challenge, Hoyle agreed to try.

Thomasville Chair Company's dean of designers, Thomas Johnson, designed a reproduction of a Duncan Phyfe armchair and the Salem Steel Company of Winston-Salem fashioned a steel skeleton of his design. Harvey fitted wire mesh over the frame and began coating it, a spoonful at a time, with a mixture of cement and granite dust. It took six months to apply this mixture to a thickness of a half inch. The chair was then painted to look as if it were made of wood and upholstered with a striped material.

In the meantime, the Chamber built a base for the chair, laying the cornerstone on January 9, 1951. A timebox, embedded inside the cornerstone, contains among other things, a Bible, photos, a safety razor, a city directory, brochures, and a letter from then-mayor Harry Finch.

Mounted on its pedestal, the chair stands thirty feet tall. In 1960, it gained national attention when vice-presidential candidate Lyndon Johnson greeted supporters from atop the chair while on a campaign stop. The chair has also hosted governors, university presidents, mayors, and beauty queens. It's even been listed in *Ripley's Believe It or Not*.

Today, the Big Chair is a big Thomasville attraction, drawing attention to the town's top industry. Thomasville likes to lay claim to the World's Largest Chair, conveniently ignoring the actual World's Largest Chair in Anniston, Alabama, which stands thirty feet tall without a pedestal. Still, Thomasville's Big Chair is impressive. You can see it in its place of honor in downtown Thomasville.

Strange Statues

Big Chests • High Point

High Point, which is wall-to-wall furniture manufacturers, bills itself as the Home Furnishings Capital of the World. The town has not one, but two, count 'em, two, great big gigantic chests of drawers.

The first chest was built in the 1920s by the High Point Chamber of Commerce. A twenty-foot tall building, complete with brass knobs, it served as the town's "bureau" of information. A 1996 renovation converted it to a thirty-eight foot tall Goddard-Towsend (whatever that is) block front chest. The real chest that was used as a prototype can be viewed in the lobby of the local visitor information center. As a finishing touch, two huge socks dangle from a middle drawer, symbolizing the town's hosiery industry.

The second chest is even more impressive. Built by Furnitureland South Mart, this eighty-five-foot tall, forty-foot wide bureau is attached to the store's entrance. The American Colonial Highboy is complete with brass pulls.

High Point is home to two gigantic chests of drawers.
Courtesy of High Point CVB.

The Goodard Block Front is located at the intersection of Hamilton and Westwood streets. The Highboy is located off Interstate-85 at exit 118, then west on Business Loop 85.

BIG PIG • CHAPEL HILL

Crook's Corner Restaurant is almost as famous for its big pink pig as it is for its down-home Southern cooking. It's no surprise, I'll bet, that the specialty of the house is barbecue. The wooden pig, which soars on a platform above the restaurant entrance, was carved by local artist Bob Gaston and has earned the restaurant the nickname "The Pink Pig."

Located at 610 West Franklin Street.

Crook's Corner Restaurant's wooden pig sign has earned the restaurant its nickname, "The Pink Pig."
Courtesy of Katherine Walton.

CAPTAIN OTWAY BURNS • BURNSVILLE/SWANSBORO

Captain Otway Burns was one of North Carolina's most skillful and famous maritime heroes. A shipbuilder, he became a sailing master, plying the trade waters around Baltimore, Portland, New York, Philadelphia, and Boston. When the War of

Strange Statues

1812 erupted, he volunteered his services, operating his schooner, the *Snap Dragon*, as a privateer, preying on British ships and trade.

During his exploits, Burns exhibited extraordinary bravery and ingenuity, carrying out some of the most profitable raids in naval history. His many deeds made him a legend in his own time and earned him a reputation as North Carolina's most famous hero of the war.

After the war, Burns returned to shipbuilding in Swansboro, where he built the *Prometheus*, the first steamship to be built in North Carolina. From 1821 until 1835, he represented Carteret County in the General Assembly. However, his sense of fairness cost him that position when he joined forces with Bartlett Yancey and John "Yellow Jacket" Bailey and cast the tie-breaking vote to increase representation of North Carolina's western counties in the General Assembly, a move that helped to create Yancey County.

In gratitude, Bailey donated land for the county seat and requested that it be named Burnsville. In 1836, President Andrew Jackson appointed Burns keeper of Brant Shoals Lighthouse in Portsmouth. He died at age seventy-five in Portsmouth in 1850 and was buried in the Old Burying Ground in Beaufort. A cannon from the *Snap Dragon* rests atop his tomb.

Today, there are two towns named in his honor—Burnsville in Yancey County and Otway in Carteret County. There are also two statues of the esteemed hero. One sits atop a forty-ton granite pedestal in the center of Burnsville's public square. This statue was given to the county on July 5, 1909, by grandson

Walter Burns. The second statue stands in sight of the sea in Swansboro.

COFFEE POT • WINSTON-SALEM

If you need a cuppa joe, mosey on over to Winston-Salem, where a twelve-foot high, sixteen-foot-around coffee pot has become a beloved symbol of the city.

The coffee pot dates back to 1858, when tinsmith Julius Mickey first opened a shop on the corner of Main and Belews streets. A competitor opened down the street, and Mickey adorned his shop with the giant coffee pot to distinguish between the two. But its location outside the store posed a traffic hazard, which was worse once cars came into popular use. Finally, a car knocked the pot from its perch and city aldermen refused to let it be replaced citing concern for public safety.

It rusted at the back of the store until its position was threatened by a proposed expressway. As a result, it was relocated on a grassy plot at the point where the Old Salem by-pass enters Main Street, where it sits today.

Throughout the years, legends have arisen about the pot. According to one story, a Confederate soldier hid himself inside the pot and avoided certain death from Union troops. It's also said that when federal troops led by General George Stoneman rode through Salem in 1865, they were met on the outskirts of town and led to the coffee pot, where they were then served coffee.

There's also a story that says the coffee pot served as a mail drop for a British spy during the Revolutionary War, but if you fall for that one, we've got some oceanfront property you might be interested in, 'cause, if you'll remember, the pot was crafted in 1858—almost a hundred years after that particular skirmish.

You can get a gander at Winston-Salem's giant coffee pot at the junction of South Main Street, Old Salem Road, and Brookstown Avenue.

CONCRETE LEGS • HENDERSON

It seems that backhoe operator Ricky Pearce has a bit of the artist in him. Several years ago, inspired by the video of Marilyn Monroe standing over a street vent with her skirt billowing around her legs, he built a set of concrete legs, sans skirt. Using a crane, he placed the forty-ton, seventeen-foot-tall legs, complete with anklet and garter, in his front yard. Conveniently located on Welcome Avenue, the legs make it look as if the Jolly Green Giant's lady friend is lying in the hedges, with just her naked legs protruding. Strategically placed bushes and a set of concrete high heels placed nearby complete Pearce's slightly risque tableau.

Some of Pearce's neighbors are up in arms about his concrete legs. Citing their nearness to two churches, they raise their eyebrows and tsk, tsk. Others, however, think the legs lend a certain panache to the neighborhood. As for Pearce, he's pleased that folks come from far and wide to view his "leg work." Despite complaints, city and county officials say the legs are breaking no laws, so they'll stay put until Pearce decides to remove them. So next time you're in Henderson, drive by and take a gander at the giant gams.

Located at 525 Welcome Avenue.

CRYING TIRE BABY • RURAL HALL

If you're an ice cream lover, no doubt you're familiar with Mayfield Dairy, maker of that delectably delightful concoction, Moose Tracks. If you're not familiar with the company, fear not. Mayfield is on its way to your city with its mascot, a bodaciously buxom bovine that travels by trailer to spread word of the company's sweet products. The big cow stands about eight feet tall, and when she's not traveling, she stands outside the dairy's headquarters in Athens.

Attached to a trailer, the Crying Tire Baby helps advertise Mayfield Dairy.
Courtesy of Roadsidenut.com.

Located at 211 Water Country Parkway.

DALE EARNHARDT STATUE • KANNAPOLIS

You'd think NASCAR driving would be pretty easy, wouldnja? You just get on the track and keep turning left. And go fast. Very, very fast. Yeah, so there's a little more to it than that. It takes skill. It takes finesse. It takes guts.

Legendary driver Dale Earnhardt had all three, in spades. Earnhardt began his racing career in 1975 in NASCAR's formative years. You might say the two grew up together.

By 1979, Earnhardt began setting the track afire with his aggressive driving style, which whipped fans into a frenzy and eventually won him the title of The Intimidator. That year he beat out one of NASCAR's strongest ever field of rookies for the Rookie of the Year award. The next year, he beat tough veteran Cale Yarbourgh to win the

Dale Earnhardt was one of NASCAR's best drivers.
Courtesy of Walker-Marketing.

Winston Cup Series Championship, making him the only driver to ever win consecutively Rookie of the Year and a series championship.

From there, Earnhardt kept hitting the track, turning left, and never looking back. He racked up seventy-six career wins, which included every major racing crown, and seven Winston Cup Series Championships. He also was a four-time IROC Champion, was named one of NASCAR's 50 Greatest Drivers, and won a career total of more than forty million dollars.

In 2001, he was again poised for a winning season and there was much talk of the possibility of an unprecedented eighth

Winston Cup Championship. But tragedy struck on February 18. In the last lap of the Daytona 500, Earnhardt, who many said was holding back to allow son Dale Earnhardt Jr. and team mate Michael Waltrip to vie for the win, was struck from behind by another car. His car smashed into the wall, killing him on impact.

The NASCAR world was devastated. Fans mourned him as deeply as they would a family member and their grief has yet to subside.

Those wanting to pay homage to their hero can visit his hometown of Kannapolis, where there are two tributes to The Intimidator. Inside the Dale Earnhardt Plaza on Dale Earnhardt Boulevard, there stands a nine-hundred-pound, nine-foot-tall bronze statue. The statue faces Earnhardt's homeplace and what's known as the Idiot's Circle. This is the area where Earnhardt supposedly learned to drive and first showed a talent for turning left.

The plaza and the statue are imbued with the numerology of Dale Earnhardt's career. You'll note the number 7 is used prominently in the stairs, the statue, and the seats. Benches and flowers are in that special number 3.

Located in Dale Earnhardt Plaza, near the intersection of Dale Earnhardt Boulevard and Highway 3.

Dinosaur • Wilson

There's a fiberglass dinosaur guarding the entrance of Wilson's Imagination Station, a science and technology center. The center features more than two hundred hands-on exhibits related to space, health, the environment, and other subjects.

Strange Statues

Located inside the Historic Wilson Federal Courthouse at 224 East Nash Street.

DOGNY • RALEIGH

Our country's search and rescue dogs played a vital role in the aftermath of September 11. Thanks to their efforts, many families obtained some measure of closure in the loss of their loved one.

On the first anniversary of September 11, the American Kennel Club (AKC) commissioned a charitable public-art initiative titled "DOGNY: America's Tribute to Search and Rescue Dogs" to honor these heroes of September 11 and to raise funds for future projects. More than one hundred life-size sculptures of the dogs were displayed throughout New York City and later auctioned off with proceeds going to canine search and rescue organizations across the country.

The lobby of Raleigh's AKC Operations Center sports three DOGNY sculptures. One is a bronze sculpture of a champion German Shepherd. The other two, made of fiberglass, depict a German Shepherd painted like a flag, and a German Shepherd with a red heart painted on his left breast.

Located at 5580 Centerview Drive.

FALLEN FIREFIGHTERS MEMORIAL • RALEIGH

In May 2006, the city of Raleigh unveiled a monument to honor North Carolina firefighters who lost their lives in the line of duty. The huge monument, made of brick and bronze, depicts a firefighter trapped beneath a pile of debris, with three of his colleagues working to free him. One comforts and calls for help. Another is lifting a beam from the fallen firefighter, and one is battling the approaching blaze.

The idea for the memorial and the funds to complete it came from the North Carolina Fallen Firefighters Foundation, a group of North Carolina firefighters wishing to honor their own. Designed and sculpted by North Carolina artist Carl Regutti, the larger-than-life monument is made of brick and bronze. A granite wall backdrop lists the names of the 164 North Carolina firefighters that have died in the line of duty since 1902. Each year, the new names of fallen firefighters will be added.

Located within Nash Square at 227 West Martin Street.

FIREHORSE FRED • NEW BERN

Firehorse Fred has lost his head. But we found it. It's in the Fireman's Museum in New Bern.

Firehorse Fred was a vital member of the New Bern fire department in the early 1900s. It was his job to get the fire engine and the firemen to the fire, and he took his job seriously.

In 1925, an alarm came in and Firehorse Fred was quickly harnessed. As always, he broke from the firehouse in a dead run, pushing as hard as he could. But before he could make it to the call, which turned out to be a false alarm, he collapsed in the street. His powerful heart had finally given out.

Firehorse Fred was much loved and valued in New Bern. How to honor him? The firemen cut off his head and stuffed it, keeping it in a place of honor, no doubt, at his old fire station until 1957. That's when the Fire Museum was built and Firehorse Fred found a new home. Mounted in an attractive glass case, it still holds a place of honor there, amid the vintage fire trucks.

Located at 408 Hancock Street.

GENERAL NATHANAEL GREENE • GREENSBORO

General Nathanael Greene and the Battle of Guilford Courthouse played a vital role in the victory of the Americans in the Revolutionary War, despite the fact that the battle was technically a loss.

The battle began in the morning of March 15, 1781, and raged for two and a-half hours. During the climax of the battle, American and British forces were engaged in hand-to-hand contact. Cornwallis later commented about this battle, "I've never seen such fighting since God made me. The Americans fought like demons."

This ferociousness may have been a factor in a fateful act by Cornwallis. Against the advice of his generals, Cornwallis ordered grapeshot to be fired into the melee, killing Americans and British indiscriminately.

This decision was key to events that followed. Many British—fully a quarter of Cornwallis's forces—were killed in the battle and during the rain of grapeshot. The Americans broke off, however, and left the field with their forces largely intact, able to fight again.

Cornwallis's forces were weakened, so though the battle was a technical victory, it was costly. The loss in forces, combined with Cornwallis's mistake in abandoning his North Carolina holdings to attempt to take Virginia, resulted in the eventual British surrender at Yorktown on October 19, 1781.

To honor the intrepid and astute General Greene, Guilford Courthouse was renamed Greensboro. The

General Nathanael Greene played a vital role in the Battle of Guilford Courthouse.
Courtesy of NPS.

220-acre battlefield is preserved in the Guilford Courthouse National Military Park, the country's first park to be established at a Revolutionary War site. Reigning supreme over the park is a large pedestal-mounted statue of Greene astride his trusty steed. The statue was unveiled in 1915 to honor Greene and his American soldiers.

Located at 2332 New Garden Road.

GEORGE WASHINGTON • RALEIGH

The pride and joy of the North Carolina State Capitol building is an unusual sight: George Washington in a toga.

The North Carolina legislature hired Antonio Canova, then recognized as the world's most talented sculptor, to sculpt a statue of the country's first president to place in the rotunda of the new state capitol. Its unveiling caused quite a stir among North Carolinians, who first thought Washington should have been wearing his general's uniform. The statue soon became a source of pride for the state, however, and it was much mourned when a fire destroyed it in 1831. In 1970 a copy was finally sculpted and placed in the Rotunda, where it sits today.

See it at One East Edenton Street.

A statue of George Washington wearing a toga stands in the North Carolina State Capitol.
Courtesy of North Carolina State Capitol, Division of State Historic Sites.

North Carolina was the birthplace of three American Presidents. Andrew Jackson, the seventh President, was born in the Waxsaws area on the border of North and South Carolina. James K. Polk, the eleventh President, was born in Mecklenburg County. And Andrew Johnson, the seventeenth President, was born in Raleigh, where he later apprenticed as a tailor.

GIANT CIGARETTE • CHADBOURNE

Having a nicotine fit? Well, hie on over to Chadbourne, where you'll find the biggest cigarette you've ever seen. It even smokes!

Located on Route 410.

GIANT MILK CARTON • MOUNT AIRY

Got moo juice? North Carolina is home to a really big carton that will hold all the moo juice you can drink. Built in the 1940s, the carton stood in front of Coble Dairy. It has changed several times since then, once advertising the Flav-O-Rich Dairy, and now PET Milk. The revolving metal carton and stand measure twenty feet, but just the carton itself is twelve feet high. The shape resembles a half-gallon size carton, but we bet it'll hold more.

The Giant Milk Carton rotates in front of the PET Milk Dairy.
Courtesy of Greater Mount Airy Chamber of Commerce.

Located at 594 North Andy Griffith Parkway.

MUFFLER MEN OF NORTH CAROLINA

What is this obsession with muffler men? Maybe it's the square jaw. Maybe it's that he's just so darn tall. We don't know, but whatever it is, there are a few good muffler men in North Carolina to assuage your craving.

Asheville has a couple of muffler men dressed up like Indians. One stands in front of a local Cadillac dealership and the other guards over Erwin High School in the Leicester suburb. Twenty-five-feet tall, both wear painted-on leather breeches and moccasins and are sporting full Native American headdresses.

Cherokee's Big Indian is identical to Asheville's. He beckons visitors into a local souvenir shop.

Edneyville has a couple of big guys to see. Two are located at the Bub Hyder Ranch, where owner, Bub, has recreated a small western town. There's an Indian and a Paul Bunyan muffler man here. There's also an Old Pioneer Statue located near a farm building on Old Clear Creek Road.

Pioneer Daniel Boone is honored in Hillsborough at Daniel Boone Village, where a giant statue of the big man himself stands atop the mall building. Ok, they say it's ol' Dan'el, but we ain't so sure. This guy's wearing a floppy old hat and he sure is holdin' ol' Tick-Licker funny. Kinda sissy-like.

Lexington has the twin to Hillsborough's Daniel Boone, but they're not trying to pass him off as a hero. Nope, Lexington's Billy Bob is a plow boy. He's made of fiberglass and was reportedly made by the Unique Fiberglass Company of North Carolina, which mass-produced the statues they called The Big Man until 1980, when the mold was broken. Billy Bob stands atop Bill's Truck Stop, and though he's not holding anything, his hands are raised in the same fashion as Hillsborough's Daniel Boone. Looks kinda like the two might go off dancin' together.

Raleigh's Muffler Man is quite the sport. Once the shill for a decorating store, he's now privately owned. The owner considers him art, and periodically repaints him, changing the colors of his outfits each time. He's located on Highway 401.

Whoo Whoo! Rocky Mount's Muffler Man is a girl! And she's wearing Daisy Dukes and reportedly sporting a belly ring. She reigns over the Men's Night Out entertainment complex outside of Rock Mount. You boys better behave yourselves!

There's another big guy in Wilson. He stands atop White's Tire Company on Forest Hills Road.

VIRGINIA DARE • ROANOKE ISLAND

You may remember the story of Virginia Dare from American History class. It all started in 1587, when Sir Walter Raleigh sponsored a group of 150 men, women, and children in the establishment of a colony on Roanoke Island—the second to be established here. The first colony, consisting only of men, had failed, with many dying and others abandoning the colony to return to England.

The settlers knew when they agreed to come that conditions would be harsh here in the wilderness of the New World. They would face hostile Indians, dangerous wild animals, and the possibility of starvation, but Raleigh's promise of more than five hundred acres of land was an enticing lure for these adventuresome souls. So they brought their wives, their children, and their hope for a new life. Among those new settlers, were John White, who was appointed governor; his pregnant daughter, Eleanor; and her husband, Ananias Dare.

Strange Statues

The new colony was called the City of Raleigh of Virginia. A milestone was reached on August 18, 1587, when the first child of English descent was born to Eleanor and Ananias Dare. The beautiful, blonde-haired, blue-eyed little girl was named Virginia.

A statue of Virginia Dare is located at Elizabethan Gardens.
Photo by John W. Randal.

Just one month later, Governor White reluctantly left for England for more supplies for the colony and to recruit more settlers. He left orders that, should they find it necessary to leave the colony, the colonists should carve their destination on a tree or pole. If they were forced to leave under duress, he said, they should carve a Maltese cross above their destination.

White was detained by the war and lack of funds, but returned three years later to find the settlement abandoned. The only clue was the word CROATOAN carved into a wooden post. Since no Maltese cross was carved above it, White hoped the colonists had, for some reason, gone to join the friendly Croatoan tribe. He and some men from the fleet searched the island but found nothing.

They made plans to sail for the island of the Croatoan tribe, but bad weather forced them to return to England. Unable to finance another search, White died without ever learning the fate of his daughter or granddaughter.

A statue of Virginia Dare graces the grounds of Roanoke Island's Elizabethan Gardens, located within Fort Raleigh Historic Site, three miles north of the town of Manteo.

Natural and Manmade Wonders

Wackiness abounds on the byways of our Strange But True North Carolina. No sappy theme parks here. Instead there's a weird hodgepodge of natural and manmade wonders. You can worship in the extremes—from one of the world's smallest churches to the world's largest ten commandments—visit a dinosaur garden and a rock that blows, then scare the wits out of yourself on a mile-high swinging bridge.

BARNEY THE BEAR AND JASPER THE MONKEY • FORT BRAGG

Discovered as an orphan cub, Barney, a small Malayan Sun Bear, lived quite an exciting life as the mascot of Company Alpha, 5th Special Forces Group, Airborne in Ben Hoi, South Vietnam.

Sgt. Jerald Hilleson was especially fond of the little bear, and when his tour ended, he decided to smuggle him home with him. He got the little feller drunk and stuffed him into his duffel bag, wedging it into the overhead bin of the 727 back to the states. Well, guess what? Yep, Barney woke up over the Pacific, hung over and in a bear of a mood. By the time Sergeant Hilleson had calmed him down, he'd caused several thousand dollars worth of damage and almost got Hilleson kicked out of the Army.

Natural and Manmade Wonders

Hilleson moved Barney in at Fort Bragg, but, unfortunately, the strange weather proved fatal to the little bear. He succumbed to pneumonia in just two years. Heartbroken, Hilleson decided to stuff the little guy, despite his lack of experience in taxidermy. When he donated Barney to the fort's Special Warfare Museum, people soon began complaining about the bad smell.

But Barney was a base legend, so the museum folks didn't feel they could just toss him out. So, they sealed him in a Plexiglas box and set him up as an exhibit. Also on display at the museum is Jasper the sentinel monkey. He and others like him played an important watchdog role in the Vietnam War. When they smelled the Viet Cong approaching, they would spit as a warning.

You can see them both in the JFK Special Warfare Museum on the corner of Ardennes Road and Marion Street.

THE BILTMORE ESTATE • ASHEVILLE

Back in 1888, George Vanderbilt II, the youngest grandson of business tycoon Commodore Cornelius Vanderbilt, had a vision of a grand winter estate on a scale that would rival the summer homes built by his older brothers and sisters. It was a family tradition, this penchant for building lavish homes.

As an international traveler, intellectual, and extremely rich kid, George Vanderbilt could have built his little country retreat anywhere in the world, but in all his travels, he had not found a place more beautiful or more desirable than Asheville, North Carolina. He had made regular visits here with his mother for many years and had fallen in love with the breathtaking scenery and the mild climate.

Vanderbilt's vision was to replicate the working estates of England, a concern that would sustain itself and become a benefit to the community. He planned to name the home the Biltmore—"Bilt" the name of the Dutch town of his ancestors, and "more," the old English word for open, rolling land. Purchasing 125,000 acres, some of which are now

The Biltmore Estate was built by George Vanderbilt II.
Photo by Bill Russ.
Courtesy of NC Tourism.

occupied by the Pisgah National Forest, he then hired popular society architect Richard Hunt to design the plans. Hunt had designed homes for other Vanderbilt family members and knew the sumptuous style they preferred.

Vanderbilt's Biltmore House was designed as an imitation of the Chateau de Blois, an early sixteenth-century French chateau of the Loire Valley. A man of the future, Vanderbilt insisted on his ornate home having all the most modern high-tech marvels, including electricity, central heating, running hot and cold water to upstairs baths, mechanical refrigeration, an elevator, an electric communication system to call servants, and even a swimming pool with underwater lighting. Then he filled it with a collection of more than seventy thousand pieces that reflected Vanderbilt's style and interests. The majority of these items grace the home today.

As part of his plan to make the estate profitable, Vanderbilt commissioned Frederick Olmstead, the landscape architect who had designed New York's Central Park and the U.S. Capitol grounds, to develop the estate's lands. A pioneer in conservation, Olmstead suggested constructing a combination of a 250-acre pleasure park surrounded by a commercial timber forest. Renovation of the forest was accomplished by Gifford Pinchot, who later established the U.S. Forest Service.

Biltmore Estate was formally opened on Christmas Eve 1895 with a grand party for friends and relatives and featured a forty-foot tree, a tradition that survives today. At 175,000 square feet, Biltmore was—and still is—the largest private home in the United States. There are 250 rooms, with thirty-four master bedrooms, forty-three bathrooms, sixty-five fireplaces, three kitchens, a bowling alley, a gym, and, of course, that indoor swimming pool.

In 1898, Vanderbilt married Edith Stuyvesant Dresser and brought his young bride to her new home, where he had already completed a private suite for her. George and Edith loved entertaining family and friends in their opulent mountain retreat. The estate was constantly alive with music and laughter. The couple also felt a responsibility to the community they had adopted as home and its people. The estate employed hundreds of locals on its working farms and a commercial timber operation with its own mill. The Vanderbilts gained a reputation as excellent employers.

Vanderbilt's intense interest in forestry and farming led him to introduce new farming techniques and to found the Biltmore Forest School, the nation's first institute for scientific forestry. The couple started Biltmore Industries to teach traditional handcrafts, such as woodworking and weaving, and Edith started the School for Domestic Science to train young women in housekeeping skills. These training opportunities allowed local people to earn higher wages.

Today, Biltmore's beloved estate is one of America's show palaces. It can be seen every day of the year at One Approach Road.

BLOWING ROCK • BLOWING ROCK

Wanna know why the blowing rock blows? The blowing rock is really an immense cliff four thousand feet above sea level, formed more than one million years ago. The cliff

Blowing Rock is four thousand feet above sea level.
Courtesy of the Blowing Rock.

overhangs the Johns River Gorge, which plunges three thousand feet below. The sheer rocky walls of the gorge form a flume that channels the northwest wind straight up the cliff with such force that light objects thrown down will blow back up and over the cliff.

OK, that's the scientific version. Now the legend.

Seems way back when, a Chickasaw chieftain was disturbed by the attraction between his beautiful young daughter and a white man. Stumped as to how to resolve the situation, he brought her far away from their native plains to Blowing Rock and the care of a squaw mother.

One day the maiden was daydreaming atop the cliff and saw a Cherokee brave wandering in the wilderness below. She playfully shot an arrow in his direction. Her flirtation caught his attention and the next day he turned up on her tepee step, heart in hand. The two courted, with him singing her songs of his homeland.

One day a strange reddening of the sky brought the maiden and her brave to the high cliff. The brave saw the reddening as an omen—he must return to his tribe in the plains. She begged him not to go. Torn between love of the maiden and loyalty to his people, the brave leapt from the cliff.

Heart-broken, the maiden begged the Great Spirit to return her love to her arms. Finally one day, under a reddening sky, a mighty wind blew the brave back into her arms. And, from that day forward, a perpetual wind has blown over Blowing Rock.

Anyway, the phenomenon of Blowing Rock is mentioned in *Ripley's Believe It or Not*. Seems because of the mysterious winds,

Blowing Rock is the only place in the world where snow falls upside down. Whoa! That blows!

Located at Highway 321 South near the town of Blowing Rock.

CHEROHALA SKYWAY • ROBBINSVILLE

It took thirty-eight years to complete the fifty or so miles of this mountain skyway, named for the Cherokee National Forest in Tennessee and the Nantahala National Forest in North Carolina. It was worth the wait.

The ridge route connects Robbinsville, North Carolina, to Tellico Plains in Tennessee. On the North Carolina end, the route looks down on the Appalachian Mountains, and the Snowbird, Slickrock, and Joyce Kilmer forests. On a clear day, you can see as far as the Great Smoky Mountains. On the Tennessee end is the splendor of the Cherokee National Forest, including Bald River Falls and the Tellico River.

Climbing to elevations of more than 5,400 feet, this National Scenic Byway winds through some of

Cherohala Skyway is approximately fifty miles long.
Courtesy of Ron and Nancy Johnson.

the most spectacular mountain scenery in the world. Fall is an especially beautiful time, with red, yellow, and orange foliage painting the mountains in a fiery blaze.

About twenty-two miles out of Tellico Falls is the Charles Hall Bridge, a seven-hundred-foot bridge at a four-thousand-foot elevation. A breathtaking ride, it's one of the highest bridges in the Southeast and is named for the man most responsible for the building of the skyway.

Stock up and fill the chariot before leaving, for though there are rest stops along the way, there are no gas stations and no restaurants through the whole of the skyway.

CHIMNEY ROCK • CHIMNEY ROCK

Chimney Rock is a giant monolith that rises 2,800 feet into the air. It's stately. It's beautiful. But, of course, it could be better.

See, we could blast a shaft through it and add an elevator. Then at the top we can put a lounge. Oh! And a snack bar! Yeah, that's just what it needs.

Without all that, Chimney Rock is just a giant rock. True, it's 315

Visitors can climb four hundred steps to enjoy the view from Chimney Rock.
Photo by Bill Russ.
Courtesy of NC Tourism.

feet across and it's got panoramic views of lakes, waterfalls, and the surrounding Blue Ridge Mountains. But what's that compared to a mile-high gift shop filled with kitschy souvenirs?

There are two ways to get to the top of Chimney Rock. You can take the twenty-six-story elevator to the top. Or if you're in need of your exercise, you can take the stairway to heaven. It's over four hundred steps, though, so be sure to workout first.

Located on Highway 64/74A, near Chimney Rock.

Tryon, North Carolina's *Tryon Daily Bulletin* is billed as the World's Smallest Daily. The page size of the paper is 8.5 inches by 11 inches.

CLINGMAN'S DOME • BRYSON CITY

At 6,643 feet, Clingman's Dome is the highest point of the Appalachian Trail and the second highest point in the state. The mountain was named for prospector Thomas Clingman, who became wealthy on the timber and minerals of the region and who was later a Civil War General and U.S. Senator.

You can hike to the top via a half-mile paved trail. Watch the weather, though, and bring a sweater, for it can snow on the dome anytime between December and April and temperatures are usually fifteen degrees cooler at the top.

As you hike, you may notice many dead Spruce Fir trees, which have been attacked by the Balsam Woolly Adelgid. This hungry little insect was brought into the country by accident in the 1800s. It migrated to the South from New England in the 1980s and devastated the older Spruce Firs.

Natural and Manmade Wonders

Clingman's Dome is open year around, but the park closes from December 1 to April 1 or whenever there's a snowfall, allowing hiking or cross country skiing up the seven-mile trail from the gate to the Dome.

Located on the state line between North Carolina and Tennessee. Follow US 441, then take Clingman's Dome Road to the parking area.

CONFEDERATE IRONCLADS • KINSTON

At the onset of the Civil War, Confederate naval officials knew a lack of time and resources prevented the construction of a naval fleet to rival the U.S. Navy's. Convinced the way to overcome this deficiency was to quickly build a small fleet of ironclads, Stephen Mallory, the Confederate Secretary of Navy, began an aggressive shipbuilding program.

Unfortunately, iron was a scarce commodity in the South after the ore fields of Tennessee and Kentucky were captured by Union troops. Even when the iron was available, getting it where it was needed became a huge problem because the railways were commandeered to move troops and supplies to other areas.

Resourcefulness became a key to acquiring the iron needed to build the ironclads. In early November 1862, Secretary Mallory showed his ingenuity by appealing to North Carolina Governor Zebulon Vance to allow the Navy to take up the rails of useless railroad routes and use the iron in ship construction, an appeal the governor heeded.

North Carolina native Commander James Cooke, charged

with overseeing the construction of ironclads in North Carolina, showed ingenuity as well. Reportedly, the boiler of the CSS *Neuse*, named for the river on which it was constructed, came from Engine 34 of the Baltimore and Ohio Railroad and her engine came from a saw mill in New Bern.

Despite this ingenuity, the delays in construction proved fatal for the *Neuse*. The shipbuilders constantly had to dodge Union troops passing through the town of Whitehall, where its construction was taking place.

Confederate Ironclads such as this were part of the Confederacy's aggressive shipbuilding program.
Courtesy of Andrew Duppstadt.

Then in November 1863, the wooden *Neuse* was slipped into the Neuse River and was poled eighteen miles downstream to Kinston for its transformation into an ironclad. However, difficulties in getting the iron plating to Kinston resulted in serious construction delays, and it was late April before the ship was completed.

On April 22, 1864, the ironclad CSS *Neuse* finally set off on its maiden voyage to take on the Yankees at New Bern, but it sailed only a half mile before becoming stuck fast on a sandbar, where it stayed until a sudden rainstorm enabled her to free herself and return to her port at Kinston.

Because of the delay in construction, which saw the ship trying to leave the Neuse River at a time when the river was too shallow, New Bern—and numerous lives—were lost to the Yankees. The river didn't rise sufficiently until November, at which time, a lack of ground support forced the ship to remain idle until March of the next year.

By the time the captain was able to get the ship into service, Union troops had advanced to within five miles of Kinston and were engaged in the Battle of Southwest Creek. Realizing it was hopeless to try to make it the sixty miles downriver to New Bern, the ship's captain shelled Union troops with the ship's cannons. He then ordered his men to place a charge under the bow and set fire to the ship in order to prevent its capture. The explosion blew an eight-foot hole in the port side and sent the *Neuse* to the river bottom.

The ship languished there in the mud for nearly one hundred years. In 1963, the ship's hull was raised and transported to a place of honor at the Caswell-Neuse Historic Site. Nearly fifteen thousand artifacts were recovered from the Neuse, one of the largest collections of a Confederate ship in the country. A portion of the artifact collection is on display at the Visitor Center of the Caswell-Neuse Historic Site, along with a scale model of the *Neuse*. The model features a starboard cutaway that reveals the boat's intricate interior features and armament.

Located at 2612 West Vernon Avenue.

COW PALACE • RALEIGH

Holy cow! The official name of the place is the J.S. Dorton Arena, but since its completion in 1952, it's been affectionately known as the "Cow Palace." Built as a livestock-judging pavilion for the North Carolina State Fair, the arena has been internationally acclaimed for its marriage of architecture and engineering. Its bold rounded design was conceived by Matthew Norwicki, the Polish architect who helped lay out the rebuilding of Warsaw after World War II.

When he was killed in a plane crash before construction began, local architect William Deitrick was commissioned to complete construction.

The pavilion's pioneering design, which suspended the roof from steel cables rather than using support beams, won many international design awards. In 1957, the American Institute of Architects named it one of the ten twentieth-century buildings most expected to influence the future of American architecture.

For many years, the pavilion served as the place where animals would strut their stuff for a panel of judges—a livestock beauty pageant. Today the building is used year around as the city's premier exhibition space. It was placed on the National Historic Registry in 1972.

Located at 1026 Blue Ridge Road.

EIFFEL TOWER • FAYETTEVILLE

Ooo la la! It's a tres petite slice of Paris right here in downtown Fayetteville. At just 150 feet, North Carolina's Eiffel Tower is a one-twelfth scale model of the original. It was built in 1963 and stands in the heart of Bordeaux—Shopping Center, that is.

Located at 1740-A Owen Drive.

Natural and Manmade Wonders

FIELDS OF THE WOOD • MURPHY

Wow! Finally, an attraction where we baby boomers can leave those pesky eyeglasses at home. You see, at Fields of the Wood everything comes in larger print—and we do mean larger!

Fields of the Wood was the brain child of Ambrose Jessup Tomlinson, who came from Indiana in the early 1900s to pass out religious tracts to the western North Carolina mountain people. Once

North Carolina's Eiffel Tower is a one-twelfth scale model of the original.
Courtesy of <u>The Fayetteville Observer</u>.

here, Tomlinson decided to form a new church in search of the true way to Christ. Before meeting with his followers to brainstorm the new church, Tomlinson hiked up to a nearby mountain to pray. When he returned, he said God had communicated with him and revealed what kind of church they should form. This was the beginning of the Church of God of the Prophecy, a church that now boasts of more than 700,000 members in 115 countries.

One of the missions of the church, said Tomlinson, would be to mark sacred spots, because in the Old Testament, Jacob had marked the spot where he envisioned the ladder to heaven. This mission led the church to purchase 210 acres of land, including the mountain where Tomlinson had gone to pray. It was here Tomlinson planned the holy place he called Fields of the Wood.

In keeping with that whole Moses-on-the-Mount theme, Tomlinson decided the first project should be to create the world's largest Ten Commandments. They should have concrete letters five feet tall and four feet wide and they should be splayed across the mountain where he had gone to pray.

Unfortunately, Tomlinson died in 1943, living only long enough to see the commandments spelled out in lime. They were finished in whitewashed concrete in 1945. The tableau is so large that it can be seen from orbit—and from heaven, we presume.

You can study each commandment up close as you ascend the 350-step stairway between the two tablets. Or, you can drive up the paved back driveway and peer down upon them from atop the mount.

At the top, you'll find a giant open Bible—reportedly the World's Largest Testament, inside of which is a stairway leading to an observation deck on top. There you can see a plethora of religious sights.

Located on State Highway 294, eighteen miles west of Murphy.

FONTANA DAM • GRAHAM COUNTY

Fontana Dam is a modern-day miracle. The largest dam east of the Rockies, it was begun in 1942, during the height of

Natural and Manmade Wonders

World War II, when steel and other resources were at a severe shortage.

Because it was constructed in a remote area of the state, a special railroad was built to transport supplies and a

Fontana Dam is the largest dam east of the Rockies.
Courtesy of Fontana Village.

camp was organized to house the five thousand men and women who worked three shifts around the clock, seven days a week. The accelerated schedule slashed construction time almost in half.

Military marches and big band music was piped into the camp over a public address system and bright flood lights lit up the dark hills as workers toiled through the night. Everywhere signs reminded workers of their patriotic duty to the war effort.

The massive effort broke construction records, with the dam being completed in November 1944, when the lake filled. On January 20, the first power to the area was generated. The project cost $74.7 million.

Today, at 480 feet, the Fontana Dam is the highest concrete dam east of the Rocky Mountains. It's 2,365 feet in length and generates a total capacity of 250,000 kilowatts of power.

Surrounded by the beauty of the Great Smoky Mountains, national forests, and deep river gorges, it's one of the country's most beautiful sights.

Located just off Highway 28, thirty-five miles west of Bryson City, NC.

GRAVES OF SIAMESE (OOPS! CONJOINED) TWINS • WHITE PLAINS/CHARLOTTE

Ever wonder why conjoined twins for more than a century were called "Siamese Twins?" The term originated in the 1800s, from conjoined twins Eng and Chang Bunker, who were born in Siam (now Thailand) in 1811. The twins were joined by a six-inch band of tissue that initially had them face to face. A doctor taught them how to stretch the tissue to allow them to stand side by side.

As children the twins spent some time in the court of the King of Siam—until being discovered by a visiting Scotsman, who convinced the king to allow the twins to tour the United States as a circus exhibition. The twins became famous and with the help of P.T. Barnum, they made a good living as entertainers. Their popularity introduced the phrase "Siamese Twins" to the English language.

In 1839, they visited Wilkesboro and decided to settle there. They adopted the last name "Bunker," possibly from the Battle of Bunker Hill, and became respected members of the community.

Despite their unusual situation, the twins lived a relatively normal life. In 1843, they married the lovely Yates sisters, initially setting up a household together. The sisters, however, couldn't seem to get along and they eventually set up two households just outside of Mount Airy. The twins would spend three nights at each household. The arrangement must've worked well, for between them, the twins sired twenty-two children.

In 1874, Chang contracted pneumonia and died suddenly during the night of January 17. Reportedly, the family called for a doctor to

Chang and Eng became famous while traveling with P.T. Barnum's circus.
Photo submitted by Surry Arts Council and Greater Mount Airy Chamber of Commerce.

perform an emergency separation, but Eng died three hours after Chang. The two are buried together in the White Plains Church Cemetery in Surry County's White Plains.

Now, you'd think that'd be the end of the story for conjoined twins in North Carolina. You'd be wrong. The state is the resting place for another set of famous twins. Daisy and Violet Hilton were born in 1908 in Brighton, England, to an unwed mother, who, upon seeing the twins, told the midwife to "Take the little monsters."

Mary Hilton, the midwife, saw the novelty appeal of the twins and gladly took them. She pushed them into show business and kept control of their careers and their money. At age twenty-one, they sued for and won their independence from Hilton's daughter, who had inherited the twins upon her mother's death.

The twins continued their show business careers, gaining fame and, it seems, quite a risque reputation. Unfortunately, they weren't very good money managers and by the 1960s, the sisters found themselves destitute.

They were later abandoned by their unscrupulous manager in Charlotte, where they lived until their death in 1969.

The twins are buried in the Forest Lawn Cemetery.

JOCKEY'S RIDGE SAND DUNE • NAGS HEAD

Jockey's Ridge is the tallest natural sand dune system in the Eastern United States. Depending upon weather conditions, its height varies from eighty to one hundred feet. The size and shape of the dune constantly changes, but it never blows away. During the winter, the wind usually blows from the northeast and in the summer it blows from the southeast. So, the sand just blows back and forth, keeping a relatively constant height.

An example of a medano, a huge hill of shifting sand with no vegetation, Jockey's Ridge was formed when strong water currents from hurricanes and other storms washed sand from offshore shoals onto the beach. The wind then picked up the sand and blew it inland, where, after many years, it formed a dune system that stretches miles along the coast.

Natural and Manmade Wonders

Since 1973, local groups have worked to preserve the Jockey's Ridge dune system, which has been declared a National Natural Landmark. The area is now a national park, with nature trails, picnic areas, hang-gliding, sand boarding, and water sports.

The entrance to the park is located in Nags Head at mile marker 12 on Highway 158.

KORNER'S FOLLY • KERNERSVILLE

Back in 1878, Jule Korner was a swinging bachelor in need of a swinging bachelor pad. So he decided to build himself a temporary party home, something he could also use as an office space for his fledgling interior design business. Never expecting to use the home as a permanent residence, Korner took the opportunity to showcase his various design styles, which helps to explain the house's eccentricities.

Korner planned to eventually build a larger house on the back of the property and use his old bachelor pad as a carriage house. The home started out with a carriageway and two haylofts.

As the structure was being built, a farmer passed by and commented that the result would be "Jule Korner's Folly." Korner was amused by the statement and took to calling his home by that name and even went so far as to have it set in tile in front of the house.

The house, completed (the first time) in 1880, had eleven rooms on three stories. But Korner wasn't satisfied and immediately began making changes. By his death in 1924, it had twenty-two rooms on seven stories.

None of the home's doorways are the same size. Some of the ceilings in the home are twenty-five feet high. Some are just six feet. Almost every ceiling in the house has murals painted by German master Caesar Milch.

Korner's Folly was originally completed in 1880.
Courtesy of Korner's Folly Foundation.

The home's extensive woodwork features bead details, rope work, Greek key, acanthus leaves, and paneling. None of the home's fifteen fireplaces are made from the same tile and some of the floors are tiled to look like throw rugs.

Outside the front door, you'll find the Witch's Corner, where visitors throw coins before entering on the presumption that evil spirits will be attracted to shiny things outside the house and would not be tempted to enter the house.

Korner died in 1924 and his wife, Alice, died in 1934. By the 1970s, the house had sat vacant for more than thirty years and had fallen into disrepair. It was on the verge of being condemned when a group of twenty-six Kernersville citizens stepped in. Contributing one thousand dollars each, they began renovations of Korner's Folly.

Today, Korner's Folly, billed as the strangest house in the world, is open for tours. Although it has yet to be completely

Korner's Folly may be Jule Korner's lasting legacy, but back in the day, he became famous for another endeavor. He was instrumental in North Carolina's first advertising campaign.

During the Civil War, Confederate and Union soldiers often traded goods for tobacco. At this time, brand names were rarely used, with the soldiers asking only for the "best." The Bull Durham brand sprang from an incident occurring during the last days of the war.

Seems soldiers from both sides raided the tobacco fields of a Durham farmer as they awaited the end of the war. After the war, these soldiers wrote back to North Carolina requesting more of that particular tobacco, which happened to be the brightleaf. The farmer, John Green, was happy to oblige, naming his brand Bull Durham in 1868. It later became the largest selling tobacco brand in the world.

Korner's involvement began when he was hired by Bull Durham's tobacco company to paint Bull Durham ads on buildings and landmarks throughout the world.

restored to its former glory—a fund raising effort is underway to raise the estimated $15 million it will take—it's a worthy stop on our Strange But True tour through North Carolina.

Located at 413 Main Street.

LAND OF OZ • BANNER ELK

Back in 1970, probably the most kitschy decade ever, Jack Puentes and Grover Robbins, two North Carolina visionaries, wanted to do something special for the kiddies, and oh, maybe something profitable for themselves. Theme parks were enjoying a heyday and Robbins had enjoyed success with his Tweetsie Railroad Park. So, hey! Let's do a theme park! Wizards! Witches! Munchkins! Toto!

You got it. The two decided their theme was to be *The Wizard of Oz*. They named the park Land of Oz and set about creating the Emerald City, complete with forty thousand glazed bricks paving that famous Yellow Brick Road. The guys located their park on the tippy top of Beech Mountain, a local ski resort, so their visitors' adventure began with a trip over the rainbow in Ozzy gondolas (actually a ski lift).

Once there, they trekked a short mountain trail punctuated by a fountain and gazebo-come-souvenir shop. There, they found, encased in glass, the costume worn by the Wicked Witch of the West in the 1939 MGM movie. A little further on, they came upon a Kansas farmhouse and were rushed into the storm cellar. Hurry! Hurry! The storm's a comin'! Cold wind blew through the cellar, and psychedelic lights (remember those?) gave the illusion that the house was spinning. When it stopped, visitors exited the cellar into an exact replica of the first farmhouse, only this one was all askew, with a buckled floor and broken furnishings. Afterward they traipsed down the Yellow Brick Road to the Emerald city, accompanied by all the characters of the book and movie. All in all, it was a dandy strange but true journey.

Natural and Manmade Wonders

The Land of Oz enjoyed a ten-year heyday, but by 1980, changing times and economics forced the park to close. It sat fallow, the victim of vandals and thieves until 1990, when the Emerald Mountain development began, using the concept of Oz in its development strategy.

The property became a sort of archeological dig with many of the sites being restored over the years.

Today, it's a private garden with Dorothy's farmhouse, the gazebos, and the fountain being restored. Dorothy's Cottage is now rented out for romantic weekends and every fall, Emerald Mountain stages an Autumn at Oz Party. Proceeds from the party go toward further park restoration.

Located at 2669 South Beech Mountain Parkway.

LINVILLE CAVERNS • MARION

Deep beneath Humpback Mountain lies Linville Caverns, North Carolina's only show cavern. The caverns were discovered back in the 1800s, when a group of mountain men became intrigued with schools of trout that seemed to swim out of the mountain.

The caverns were opened for touring in 1937 by owner John Gilkey, for whom one of the most spectacular cavern rooms is named. Level pathways and dramatic lighting were added to enhance the touring experience.

Some of Mother Nature's most skillful and beautiful artwork can be found in Linville caverns. The walls and ceilings sparkle with crystals and spectacular outcrops of stalactite and stalagmite, and flowstone decorate each cavernous chamber.

One horizontal formation of flowstone is so flat, tour guides refer to it as the ballroom. It's guarded by a formation that uncannily resembles an alligator. Other formations include one that looks like George Washington and one that's affectionately known as Mr. Bones, and some that look like tobacco leaves, for which North Carolina is famous.

Near the end of the caverns lies a lake so deep it's considered bottomless. Several years ago, researchers were stymied in their attempt to gauge the lake's depth when their measuring device reached its limit of 250 feet.

In addition to its interesting geological features, the cavern has an intriguing history. Civil War soldiers hid here, and traces of campfires can still be seen. Smoke from those fires unfortunately revealed their location.

Thomas Edison once sent a team here in search of platinum, once vital to the production of incandescent lamps. The gems they found earned North Carolina its reputation as a "Gem State."

Located off U.S Highway 221.

Love Valley • Fox Mountain

Wondering what an authentic western town is doing smack dab in the heart of the Deep South? Wonder no more. Seems that back in 1948, Andy Barker, the cowboy's biggest fan, wanted to live where the loudest noises were the clip clop of horses' hooves and the jingle jangle of silver spurs. There weren't no place like that 'round these parts. So, ol' Andy jest built himself that place. He named it Love Valley and, as founder, he appointed himself its first mayor.

Natural and Manmade Wonders

Love Valley is a true reproduction of a western, cowboy-type town. The streets are dirt and only feet or hooves are allowed on them. There's a dancehall and a saloon, a tack shop, a general store, and a blacksmith shop. It's a scene straight out of *Gunsmoke*. There's even a Miss Kitty's just outside of town, only it's a bed and breakfast instead of a saloon.

The town of Love Valley is open only on the weekends, but the nearby campgrounds and stables are open all week. You can bring your own hoss, or rent one when you get there.

Located on Love Valley Road in Love Valley.

MYSTERY HILL • BLOWING ROCK

Legend has it that, back in 1949, North Carolinian William Hudson discovered a mountain oddity on his property. Seems there was a gravity anomaly that caused some weird things to happen. Balls rolled up hill instead of down. Weird.

Not one to let an opportunity roll past him, Hudson developed his property, building a strangely angled building he called the Mystery House. He claimed it was the stronger-than-average pull of gravity that changed the laws of physics, allowing the ability for people to stand at a forty-five degree angle and water to flow uphill. Scientists say it's just an optical illusion.

At any rate, these and the other exhibits will make you doubt your own eyes.

Located at 129 Mystery Hill Lane.

SHELL BUILDING • WINSTON-SALEM

A slice of Americana has survived in Winston-Salem. The shell-shaped gas station, once one of eight, is now one of a kind. It was built in 1930 for the Quality Oil Company, a local Shell gasoline marketer. Constructed of bent green wood, wire, and concrete stucco, the building was built by R.H.

This shell-shaped building was built in 1930.
Photo by John Borwick.

Burton and son Ralph as an advertising ploy for Shell Oil.

The building was reincarnated as a lawn mower repair shop during the 1970s and 1980s. It had fallen into disrepair in the 1990s, when its historical value was recognized by Preservation North Carolina, a historical preservation group. The group spent fifty-thousand dollars to restore the landmark and was successful in getting it placed on the National Register of Historical Places. Preservation North Carolina has a fifteen-year lease on the building and is using it as their satellite office.

Located at on the corner of Sprague and Peachtree streets.

ST. JUDE CHAPEL OF HOPE TINY CHURCH • TRUST

St. Jude is the patron saint of lost causes. Perhaps that's what Mrs. Burutio felt like when she was diagnosed with cancer. She survived to build the tiny church to honor St. Jude. The church, which seats about eight people, is always open to visitors.

Located at the intersection of state highways 203 and 63.

Tweetsie Railroad • Blowing Rock

Tweet, tweet is a sound you expect from little yellow birds with lisps, not train whistles. The engine that routinely chugged up the mountain from Johnson City, Tennessee, to Cranberry, North Carolina, however, had a tweety whistle so shrill that the local folks dubbed the train the "Tweetsie."

The Tweetsie's history dates back to 1866, when Tennessee's legislature awarded the East Tennessee & Western North Carolina Railroad Company permission to build a railroad. The main purpose of the ET&WNC, which mountain wags dubbed Eat Taters and Wear No Clothes, was to operate from Johnson City to the ore mines of Cranberry.

Fifty miles of track were laid through the rugged mountain terrain of the Blue Ridge Mountain chain and the railroad began operations in 1881. In 1916 additional track was laid to Boone and passenger service was added, opening a formerly isolated area.

The Tweetsie was a regular and beloved fixture in the mountains until the construction of mountain roads began its decline. The floods of 1940 washed out several sections of the railroad, and, finally, on July 13, 1950, ET&WNC officially closed down. Tweetsie Locomotive No. 12, the last of the original thirteen coal-fired engines, was bought by railroad enthusiasts, who later sold it to singing cowboy and movie actor Gene Autry.

Autry planned to ship the locomotive out west and use it in films. North Carolina mountain man Grover Robbins Jr. had other plans, however. Deciding it was time for the Tweetsie to return to its old home, he approached Autry about the locomotive. Autry, having learned just how expensive it would be to ship the Tweetsie to California, was looking to unload the locomotive cheap—really cheap. He

Tweetsie Railroad was named for its shrill whistle.
Courtesy of Tweetsie Railroad.

sold it to Robbins for the grand sum of one dollar. The Tweetsie returned to its mountain home in 1956.

A celebration ensued, with the governor designating May 20, 1956, as "Tweetsie Homecoming Day." After undergoing a complete restoration, the engine and a couple of original rail cars were moved to a scenic spot near Blowing Rock and people began traveling to Blowing Rock to see the train.

Hey! thought Robbins. We might be onto something here! What we need is a theme park! Wild west train rides! Variety shows! Park rides! Yeah, that's what we need. In the summer of 1957, the Tweetsie made her first run at her new location and people came from all over the South to hear the familiar Tweet! Tweet! of the train whistle.

The Tweetsie quickly became one of North Carolina's most popular tourist attractions. Today, the locomotive makes a scenic three-mile loop through the mountains near Blowing Rock, during which the train is attacked by Indians and outlaws. Other attractions include a tilt-a-whirl and a ferris wheel.

Located on Highway 321 between Boone and Blowing Rock.

Strange Museums

There's a strong sense of history here, as evidenced by the large number of museums throughout the state. But you won't find works by Picasso or Monet gracing these walls. Nah. We're much more interesting than that.

THE AIRBORNE & SPECIAL OPERATIONS MUSEUM • FAYETTEVILLE

It wasn't long after the invention of the airplane that some nut came up with the idea to jump out of one. In the case of the U.S. Airborne forces the idea was posited in 1918 by Colonel Billy Mitchell, Commander of U.S. aviation units in France, who suggested the use of parachute troops in assault.

Though World War I ended before the idea could be implemented, it was kicked around in the years between wars, until 1940, when a Test Platoon was

The Airborne & Special Operations Museum shows the history of paratroopers.
Courtesy of ASOM.

formed to try it out. Of the two hundred adrenaline junkies who volunteered, only forty-eight made the grade.

North Carolina native William C. Lee was the first commander of the new parachute school in Fort Benning and was the first commander of the new 101st Airborne Division. Lee was awarded the Distinguished Service Medal and became known as the Father of the Airborne for his work with the country's newest weapon.

By 1942, Fort Bragg had become the largest airborne training facility in the world, sending parachute and glider forces to the Pacific and to Europe. After World War II, the airborne units of Fort Bragg became a strategic force, ready to fight anywhere in the world at a moment's notice.

Although guerrilla warfare was a common thing, the Army's Special Forces didn't get started until 1944 when 2,300 men were sent to Fort Bragg for training. Designated the 10th Special Forces Group, this first unit was activated in 1956, with the main mission "to infiltrate by land, sea, or air deep into enemy territory and organize the resistance/guerrilla potential to conduct Special Forces operations with an emphasis on guerrilla warfare." Quite an order, we'd say.

The green beret was designated in 1953 as the headgear for Special Forces troops and it was worn whenever the troops went into the field for extended exercises—although the Army refused to authorize its official use. In 1961, when President John F. Kennedy was planning to visit Fort Bragg, he sent word the Special Forces should wear their green berets for the event. He felt, since the troops had special training, they should have something to set them apart. The Army acquiesced and the green beret became the official symbol of the Special Forces.

The Airborne & Special Operations Museum at Fort Bragg details the history of the Army's elite forces from World War II until today through an array of innovative exhibits. There's also a 255-seat Vistascope theater that provides a huge, startlingly clear image of the battle, and a fifty-seat video theater offering an array of educational films.

Located at 100 Bragg Boulevard.

ALUMINUM TREE AND ORNAMENT MUSEUM • ASHEVILLE

Holy Merry Christmas, Santa Man! Could there be anything tackier than those aluminum Christmas trees of yesteryear? We think not. That's why the world's only Aluminum Tree and Ornament Museum—ATOM for short— holds such a special place in our hearts. The museum also is known as the Aluminum Tree & Aesthetically Challenged Seasonal Ornament and Research Center.

The museum got its start in 1991, when the gift of one lone tree to museum curator Stephen Jackson sparked an interest in collecting them. Jackson came up with the idea to use the museum as a fund raising effort for such causes as the Girl Scouts, student scholarships, and the Smith-McDowell House Museum. It's open annually from November until January 1.

The museum has a permanent collection of more than one hundred vintage aluminum trees, fifty to sixty of which are chosen for viewing each year. The collection includes a number of "theme" decorated trees, plus a number of celebrity trees, featuring famous personalities and icons of the twentieth century, such as Elvis and Tammy Faye Baker. Also on display are a large collection of aesthetically-challenged Christmas ornaments. Our favorites are the toilet ornaments. That copper tank ball looks so pretty against all that silver!

In the gift shop, there's a variety of aluminum tree products. Especially popular is the aluminum tree potpourri, to fill your home or car with the wonderfully fresh scent of an aluminum tree forest. And don't forget to pick up a package of aluminum tree seeds, so you can grow your own!

Located at 283 Victoria Road.

The Aluminum Tree and Ornament Museum houses a collection of over one hundred vintage aluminum trees.
Courtesy of aluminumtree.com.

Andy Griffith Museum • Mount Airy

Billed as THE WORLD'S LARGEST ANDY GRIFFITH COLLECTION, the Andy Griffith museum consists of memorabilia collected by Emmett Forrest, Griffith's childhood friend. Forrest collected the items for more than thirty years, scattering them around his Mount Airy home.

When he moved into a condo, however, there just wasn't room for THE WORLD'S LARGEST ANDY GRIFFITH COLLECTION. So, now the collection is on display at Mount Airy's Main Oak Emporium. Here, you'll find that rumpled suit Griffith wore in nearly every single episode of *Matlock*—only now it's all pressed and spiffy-looking. There's the blue canvas actor's chair with his name emblazoned on the back and album covers, scripts, and photographs.

The weirdest piece of memorabilia would have to be the orange and white plastic wrapper that once encased some Andy Griffith Whole Hog Sausage, which Griffith endorsed in the sixties. Forrest got it at a memorabilia auction. Paid $276 for it.

Located in the Main Oak Emporiumon Main Street.

Ava Gardner Museum • Smithfield

A kiss is just a kiss…Well, not to Tom Banks it wasn't. At the age of twelve, Banks was kissed on the cheek by a young woman attending secretarial school in Wilson, North Carolina. It was a kiss that inspired a lifetime of sweet devotion.

Two years later, Banks, through a newspaper photograph, learned the young woman was Ava Gardner, a rising Hollywood starlet. He began following her career and collecting all sorts of her memorabilia. He continued his obsession into adulthood, and aided and abetted by his wife, he amassed a huge collection. In the early eighties, he bought the Smithfield house where Ava lived from age two to age thirteen and opened the Ava Museum, which he operated during the summers for nine years.

Banks suffered a stroke and died in 1989—just five months before his idol, Ava, died. In 1990, his wife donated his collection to the city of Smithfield, on the promise that a permanent museum would be established in Johnson County, Ava's birthplace and final resting place.

The Ava Gardner Museum celebrates Smithfield's most famous native.
Photo by Bill Russ.
Courtesy of NC Tourism.

The museum is filled with all manner of Ava memorabilia, including photographs, a Lucien Piccard watch Ava gave to Ol' Blue Eyes, the love of her life, and a collection of portraits by Dutch artist Bert Pfeiffer. Not content to settle for Bank's collection, the museum is always in search of new items for the museum honoring Smithfield's most famous native.

Located at 325 East Market Street.

BELHAVEN MEMORIAL MUSEUM • BELHAVEN

Visit the Belhaven Memorial Museum, and you'll discover packratism taken to entirely new levels. The museum consists of thousands of items collected by Mrs. Eva Blount Way, whose obsession with collecting began in 1887, when her new mother-in-law gave her four small buttons. This small gesture sparked an interest that led to an eventual collection of thirty thousand buttons gathered from all over the world. And that wasn't all.

Miss Eva also began collecting all types of items that interested her. As friends, neighbors, and relatives learned of her obsession, they began bringing items for her to collect. By 1940, she had accumulated enough stuff to start her own museum, which she did in her own home, using the proceeds to benefit the American Red Cross.

Miss Eva had a weird streak a mile wide and along the years she managed to pick up quite a few Strange But True items. These freaky deaky exhibitions include: pickled babies in a jar, donated by the town's doctor; a two-headed kitten, a one-eyed fetal pig, a hare lipped dog, and several mummified squirrels; the dress of a seven hundred-pound woman that died in bed; and snakes killed by Mrs. Way—one is made into a necktie.

The Belhaven Memorial Museum is located on the second floor of the old Belhaven Town Hall on East Main Street.

BRADY C. JEFCOAT MUSEUM • MURFREESBORO

Wow! The sheer size of the Brady C. Jefcoat Museum will leave you speechless. The result of more than twenty-five years of collecting by Brady Jefcoat, the museum houses an amazing collection of Americana. More than eight thousand items fill room after room of the old Mufreesboro High School (built around 1922).

The collection takes you back in time and brings you forward one hundred years—from 1850 to 1950. It features the country's largest collections of butter churns, washing machine equipment, and irons. There are more than six hundred musical items, such as music boxes, a whole slew of phonographs, juke boxes, and radios.

The Brady C. Jefcoat Museum has more than eight thousand items of Americana memorabilia.
Courtesy of Upward Bound.

The largest museum in the state, the Brady C. Jefcoat Museum is a unique one-man collection. It was sought after by such prestigious institutions as the Smithsonian Institute and the North Carolina Museum of History. Jefcoat also turned down offers from London and Rome. He became acquainted with Murfreesboro when giving a commencement speech at Chowan College in 1990. After that speech, Jefcoat decided to entrust his amazing collection to the Mufreesboro Historical Association, mainly because the association convinced him they would display the collection in its entirety and they would never sell even one item, two conditions he insisted on.

Located at 201 West High Street.

COUNTRY DOCTOR MUSEUM • BAILEY

How could we possibly pass up any place that numbers a "scarificator" as one of its exhibits? No way, man! There's other cool stuff, too. Such as an amputation kit. An iron lung. An ear horn. A cupping kit—that was used to drain blood from capillaries!

The purpose of the Country Doctor Museum is to preserve the history of rural health in America. Started in 1967 by a group of ladies in Bailey who wanted to provide a lasting memorial to the rural doctors in

The Country Doctor Museum is the oldest museum in the U.S. dedicated to rural doctors.
Courtesy of the Country Doctor Museum.

their own families. It's the oldest museum in the country dedicated to this worthy cause.

Through the decades, the exhibits in the museum have grown to more than five thousand medical artifacts and six thousand historic texts collected from all over the country. You'll see examples of a doctor's examining room, and unusual equipment—including the complete amputation kit and various forms of transportation for making rounds. The exhibits also have expanded to include nursing, pharmaceuticals, and home remedies.

Located on Peele Road.

Strange Museums

DALE EARNHARDT MUSEUM • CHARLOTTE

DEI. Every NASCAR race fan knows those hallowed letters stand for Dale Earnhardt, Inc. The company was formed by Dale and his wife, Teresa, in 1980, opened in a three-bay garage with an office for Dale. As the company grew, they moved the offices into a small brick house across the street.

NASCAR's popularity was skyrocketing and Earnhardt was speeding right along with it. One of the first to recognize the marketing possibilities, he developed products emblazoned with his name and car number, a move that helped to make DEI the multi-million dollar company it is today.

By 1999, DEI had outgrown its small garage and built a seventy thousand square-foot, state-of-the-art facility that includes the garage, a showroom for the cars, gift shop, and corporate headquarters.

The place is like a shrine for No. 3 fans. Every year, thousands make pilgrimages here to pay homage. To accommodate this outpouring of affection, DEI now houses the Dale Earnhardt Museum, stockpiled with an impressive array of memorabilia. Admission is free, and as an added bonus, visitors are able to get a gander at some of DEI's hot racing machines on the six thousand-foot showroom floor.

Located at 1675 Coddle Creek Highway.

Mooresville calls itself Race City, U.S.A., because it's home to more than sixty NASCAR race teams, including some of the biggest in the sport. Indeed, North Carolina can be called the Home of NASCAR, with 90 percent of NASCAR garages headquartered in or around Charlotte.

FRANKLIN GEM AND MINERAL MUSEUM • FRANKLIN

Franklin gained the nickname the Ruby City because the pretty red stones that could be found in abundance in the Caler Fork area of the Cowee Valley. In 1893, a representative from Tiffany's of New York sent a representative to the area, and he wrote a favorable report on the value of the valley's rubies that generated interest here. Many of the locals began to send those pretty red stones and the blue ones they'd found to Tiffany's for cutting and polishing.

In 1895, a mining expert supervised work in the Cowee Valley lands and old claims purchased by the American Prospecting and Mining Company, in an effort to find the source of the valley's rubies and sapphires. They dug numerous experimental shafts and test holes, and tests were also conducted by other mining companies, but the source was never found.

In 1912 a survey by the state of North Carolina confirmed the presence of corundum, the mineral of rubies and sapphires. A hard mineral, corundum was often used as an abrasive, and in bearings and watch movements, in addition to gemstones. Though the mineral was mined for a while, no real commercial value was found, and so operations were halted in the early twentieth century.

Today many of the old mines have been reopened and adapted to gem lovers who wish to hunt for their own treasure. Some offer digging for native minerals, while others provide 'enriched sediment,' which contains minerals from other parts of the state—guaranteeing a find.

Strange Museums

After their mining expedition, novice miners can trek on over to the Old City Jail, where the Franklin Gem and Mineral Museum is housed. A trip through the museum's rooms filled with displays of raw gems and minerals will educate the new gemologists on their finds and on the geology of the state.

Located at 25 Phillips Street.

GOURD MUSEUM • ANGIER

Great giant dippers. Plates. Bowls. Baskets. The gourd is quite a useful thing.

It's also quite a popular little thingy. Believe it or not, there is an American Gourd Society, with chapters in many states, North Carolina included. There's also a gourd artist guild, dedicated to perpetuating the use of gourds as an art medium.

It's this art medium idea that makes gourds so popular. Not many varieties are good to eat, while some of them grow into shapes that even those of us who are art-challenged can see—say, a penguin, a goose, maybe a whale. True gourd artists, however, can turn a simple gourd into some pretty interesting things.

A lot of these items can be found in the Gourd Museum, which was started in 1964 by gourd enthusiasts Marvin and Mary Johnson. You'll find plenty of gourd bowls and gourd baskets, perhaps the most popular use for gourds. But you'll also find a collection of gourd musical instruments, plus whimsical gourd artwork.

The city of Angier took over the Johnson Gourd Museum collection when Marvin died in 2005. It's located at 55 N. Broad Street, where it can be viewed free of charge.

MUSEUM OF THE ALPHABET • WAXHAW

A B C D E F G...Oh, sorry. We were channeling our
kindergarten days. You will too when you visit the Museum of
the Alphabet. The museum was started by Cameron Townsend
in 1934 to "help the world come to a genuine appreciation of
the gift of writing systems."

He gives it his best effort in a 4,900-square-foot exhibition
that tells the story of alphabet makers from ancient history to
today.

Beginning with a sculpture of the Tower of Babel, a
reminder that there are six thousand languages in the world, the
museum's galleries take you through the history of many
languages and the people who developed them. Despite its
worship of the written word, the exhibition uses a variety of
media to tell its story. Photographs, paintings, sculptures,
weavings, models, and quiz boxes are all utilized to help visitors
grasp the vast amount of information disseminated.

Located at 6409 Davis Road.

MUSEUM OF THE CHEROKEE INDIAN • CHEROKEE

An Indian museum might be the last place you'd expect to
find modern-day special effects, but you'd be wrong. As you
step into the museum, you're greeted by a Cherokee storyteller
with an intriguing story to tell. Accompanied by high-tech
wizardry, your Indian guide weaves the tale of the Cherokee,
from ancient times to modern day.

You start back thousands of years, in the day of the
mastodon and progress through the rich history of our country's
native people. Learn of the Cherokee's bewilderment at the first

appearance of the white man, their participation in the Revolutionary War, and the creation of the Cherokee written language. Finally, take that sorrowful trip down the Trail of Tears.

The Museum of the Cherokee Indian celebrates Cherokee heritage.
Courtesy of Visual Terrain, Inc.

Renovated in 1998, the museum's 12,000-square-foot exhibition contains an extensive artifact collection and maintains a large archive. It's a place where you can have fun and learn, too.

Located at State Highway 441 and Drama Road.

NORTH CAROLINA MARITIME MUSEUM • BEAUFORT

Ahoy, Matey! The North Carolina Maritime Museum traces the state's extensive marine history with exhibits of boats and boat building, commercial and sport fishing, lifesaving, and marine livelihoods.

By far, the museum's most interesting exhibit is the recovery of the *Queen Anne's Revenge*, Blackbeard the Pirate's treasure ship. Blackbeard, aka Edward Teach, was North Carolina's most famous pirate. By 1718, he had teamed up with fellow pirate Major Stede Bonnet and the two began to ply the waters off the coast of the Carolinas, using a house in Beaufort, now called the Hammock House, as their headquarters. They plundered and looted and looted and plundered, generally wreaking havoc wherever they went. It was a grand life, for sure.

However, Blackbeard eventually began to weary of all that looting. It was time, he thought, to retire. North Carolina's governor, Charles Eden, had promised a pardon to any pirate who would agree to stop plundering and looting. Said pirate could settle down on a little plot somewhere in North Carolina and live a respectable life. Sounded like a plan.

One last bit of business, though. Before accepting the pardon, Blackbeard wanted to get hold of all the most valuable loot that he and Bonnet

The North Carolina Maritime Museum pays homage to the state's extensive marine history.
Courtesy of North Carolina Maritime Museum.

had spread between their two ships. His plan was a bit complicated and quite devious.

Strange Museums

First he purposely ran his ship, *Queen Anne's Revenge*, aground on a sandbar in Topsail Inlet, now known as Beaufort Inlet. Oops! He convinced Bonnet that he should send his boat *Adventurer* to help pull him back into deeper water. Double oops! Now they were both stuck.

What a pickle.

"Well, look," he told Bonnet. "You go on to Bath and pick up your pardon. I'll wait here, take care of the ships, guard the loot, and when you get back, I'll go. Then when I get back, we'll divvy up the loot and say our farewells."

Trusting soul that he was, Bonnet agreed, and taking a small boat, he sailed off to Bath Town. In the meantime, Blackbeard unloaded the loot off both ships onto a smaller ship and sailed away to get his pardon.

The *Queen Anne's Revenge* sank there in Beaufort Inlet and was lost until 1996, when a private underwater salvage company discovered a ship believed to be the *QAR* and turned the rights of excavation over to the state of North Carolina. A slow excavation is currently being performed and the museum exhibits artifacts taken from the ship.

Located at 315 Front Street.

SCOTTISH TARTANS MUSEUM • FRANKLIN

Franklin, North Carolina, might be the last place you'd expect to see guys runnin' around in plaid skirts, but that'd be afore ye learned the history of the Scottish in Franklin, indeed, mon, in the whole of the Carolinas. Both states experienced a share of Scottish immigration. In coming to

America, they brought with them their rich culture and heritage.

The tartan plays a big role in that heritage. In case you're wondering, tartan is the distinctive pattern of interlocking horizontal and vertical stripes that's often mistakenly called "plaid." Actually, the story goes, a plaid derives from "plaide," the Gaelic word for a blanket and is specifically used in the context of Highland dress to refer to a large length of material. The original kilt was known as a "belted plaid" and was basically a blanket drawn together with a belt.

Scottish heritage is alive and well at the Scottish Tartans Museum.
Courtesy of the Scottish Tartans Museum.

The earliest known Scottish tartan design dates back to the third century. It soon became extremely popular in Highland dress, so much so that in 1746 the British government, in an attempt to suppress the rebellious Scots, passed a law against the wearing of a tartan in the Highlands. As its popularity grew, the tartan patterns became individualized and took on significance, with different patterns symbolizing different Scottish clans.

The Tartans museum has more than five hundred tartans patterns on display, with a computer database of more than four thousand other patterns. The museum also has a large number of kilts, the central garment of Highland dress, on display. As an added treat, on Friday afternoons during the summer the museum's Piper-in-Residence plays the bagpipes outside the museum.

Located at 86 East Main Street.

THOMAS WOLFE MEMORIAL • ASHEVILLE

Who said you can't go home again? Oh, yeah. It was Thomas Wolfe. "Home" for the famous novelist, one of the greatest writers of the twentieth century, was a large Victorian boardinghouse in Asheville. Although the family didn't need the money, his mother, obsessed with real estate, operated the large, rambling home as a boardinghouse and used the money to buy more real estate.

Wolfe, the youngest son, never really felt comfortable in the Queen Anne Home named by a former owner "The Old Kentucky Home." He felt neglected by his mother, the single-minded businesswoman, and uncomfortable around the strangers who boarded there. He wove these experiences into his novel, *Look Homeward Angel*, published in 1929. In the book, he changed the name of the boardinghouse to Dixieland and portrayed his mother as a woman whose boarders, because of the money they represented, were more important than her children. Brutally frank about his family and the town characters he portrayed, he worried about his family's reaction, and stayed away for more than two years after its publication. As it turned out, his family was more understanding than the townspeople, who felt angry and betrayed. The book was banned from Asheville's public library for seven years.

After Wolfe's mother's death, the boardinghouse was sold to a private organization, which opened it as a memorial in 1949. Seeing the potential for a tourist attraction, the city of Asheville put aside its pique at Wolfe in 1958 and took over the memorial, running it until 1976, when it was acquired by the North Carolina Department of Cultural Resources.

The Thomas Wolfe Memorial house is preserved almost exactly as it was when Wolfe grew up there, with furnishings and accessories arranged by surviving family members. There's a visitor center and an audio-visual presentation on Wolfe's life and writings. Guided tours also are available.

Located at 48 Spruce Street.

TOBACCO MUSEUM • DURHAM

Tobacco has always been a vital part of North Carolina's economy. Even with today's anti-smoking sentiments, the state ranks number one in tobacco production, producing approximately $587 million annually.

After the Civil War, Union soldiers, having sampled Bright Leaf tobacco, the most common grown in North Carolina, began writing for more samples. Family patriarch Washington Duke planted his first crop and began a business that soon prospered. With his hard work and marketing savvy, he put Duke products on top of the industry. One of Duke's most popular products was a smoking tobacco he called "Pro Bono Publico," which translates to "For the Public Good."

Strange Museums

Well, of course, we now know how good it was for the public, but it was certainly good for the Duke family—and North Carolina's pocket book.

The invention of the cigarette machine in 1881 took tobacco sales and the family business to new heights. James Duke decided to take his product global. Taking down an atlas to check population, he settled on China—a country with 430 million potential smokers. He immediately began exporting to China and within a few years, had addicted a good portion of the population. Sales to China skyrocketed to $1.23 billion in 1902, increasing to 12 billion and $10.75 billion—with a net profit of $3.75 billion—by 1922.

In 1890, Duke convinced his four largest competitors that it would be in their best interests to merge. That year, the American Tobacco Company was formed, and Duke found himself in control of the largest tobacco industry in the world and a vast personal fortune. However, by the turn of the century, anti-monopoly sentiments forced the break up of the company. Four major tobacco companies emerged: a new American Tobacco Company, Liggett and Myers, P. Lolliard, and R.J. Reynolds.

After the break up, James Duke continued the family's business abroad. Like his father before him, he later distributed his fortune to benefit religious, medical, and educational institutions, including the endowment of Duke University.

The Duke family's influence on tobacco and North Carolina's economy is preserved in a "living history" museum, where interpreters demonstrate early tobacco farming techniques. The Duke Homestead is filled with archives and exhibits depicting the history of tobacco farming and the Duke family.

Located at 2828 Duke Homestead Road.

WRIGHT BROTHERS NATIONAL MEMORIAL • MANTEO

Twelve seconds, one hundred twenty feet. Not long. Not far. But as the first human flight, it was long enough and far enough to make history. Wilbur and Orville Wright, two bachelor brothers from Ohio, became obsessed with the conundrum of flying early on, when their father gave them a helicopter driven by rubber bands.

They took their flight at 10:35 a.m. on December 17, 1903, and stepped into history. A dispute with the Smithsonian Institute, however, delayed their entry into the books. Seems Samuel Langley, secretary of the Smithsonian, had attempted flight nine days before the Wright brothers. His flying machine broke up upon take off, unceremoniously dropping its pilot into the Potomac River.

After his death in 1906, Langley's friends at the Smithsonian worked to rehab his image, building an "exact" replica of his machine and successfully flying it. Using this as a basis and claiming that no modifications were made, the Smithsonian asserted that Langley was the first to achieve human flight.

There had been modifications, however, and Orville was so upset with the falsehoods that he sent the Wright flyer to the Science Museum in London and wrote in his will that, unless there was a change of heart, it should remain there after his death. Luckily, in 1942, the new secretary of the Smithsonian printed a retraction to the earlier claims and the flyer was brought to the Smithsonian, where it remains today.

Wright Brothers National Memorial commemorates man's first flight.
Courtesy of NC Tourism.

The Wright Brothers National Memorial is located near Kitty Hawk, where the first historic flight took place. The Visitor Center doubles as a museum with exhibits telling the story of the Wright Brothers and their historic flight. The centerpiece of the museum is a replica of the 1903 Flyer.

Sitting atop big Kill Devil Hill is the Wright Brother Memorial Tower. The sixty-foot tower is made of gray granite from nearby Mount Airy and commemorates the first flight and hundreds of glider flights that preceded the first powered flight.

There are several reconstructed 1903 buildings, one that resembles the building used as a hanger by the Wright Brothers and another similar to a workshop and living quarters. The buildings are furnished with 1900-era furnishings.

Near the reconstructed buildings, you'll find a boulder that marks the spot where the first flight left the ground. Numbered markers indicate the distance of each of the four flights made on December 17, 1903.

Located at 1401 National Park Drive.

The Haunting of North Carolina

Mist rising on moonlit nights. Ghostly apparitions floating through hallowed halls. Strange and scary noises. North Carolina can be a spooky place at night. With a past so rich in history, it's no wonder there are haints wandering our land. Here's just a smattering of North Carolina's legendary ghost tales.

Brown Mountain Lights • Burke County

Brown Mountain, located in the foothills of the Blue Ridge Parkway, may only be an unimpressive 2,600 feet high, but it's one of the country's most famous mountains. For hundreds of years, it has been the site of a mystery that has intrigued residents, visitors, and the scientific community alike, bringing international attention to North Carolina.

The Brown Mountain Lights have been seen for hundreds of years.
Photo by Lee Hawkins/Brownmountainlights.org.

The Haunting of North Carolina

The mystery that has piqued so much interest is a series of lights that appear on Brown Mountain on certain nights. They begin to appear right after dark and bob up and down the mountain. Descriptions of the lights vary, from small but brilliant balls of bobbing light to a glowing ball of fire to a bursting sky rocket to a pale, almost white, illumination. At times they pop on and off. Sometimes they drift slowly up and down the mountain, disappearing then reappearing in another spot. Other times they're said to whirl like pinwheels and dart rapidly here and there.

There are several local legends to explain these mystery lights. The first dates back to the year 1200 when Brown Mountain was inhabited by the Cherokee and Catawba Indians. In that year, a great battle was fought between the two tribes, and many people believe the lights are the spirits of young Indian maidens looking for loves lost in battle. The early frontiersmen believed the lights were the spirits of the warriors who died.

Another, more recent, legend tells of a young mountain girl living on the mountain with her father. Her father disapproved of her sweetheart, so they planned to elope and the young woman lit her torch and went out to wait for him. He never came, and many people say the light is from the torch she still carries to look for him.

The final legend concerns murder most foul. According to this legend, a wicked man named Jim, married to a woman named Belinda, began an affair with a hussy named Susie. Not long after the affair began, neighbors noticed that Belinda, who was heavily pregnant with Jim's child, had disappeared. Jim insisted she had gone to visit her mama, but folks were suspicious. A search of the couple's cabin turned up bloodstains on the living room floor. Suspicions grew when neighbors noticed an indigent stranger leaving town with Jim's horse and buggy. Could it be that he had helped kill and bury Belinda and this was his payoff?

The townsfolk instituted an extensive search for Belinda's body. Finally, one night someone noticed strange lights bobbing up and down Brown Mountain. They followed the lights and, sure enough, they were led to a spot on the mountain where they found Belinda's and her baby's bodies in a shallow grave. According to the legend, Jim escaped before he could be brought to justice, and so the lights of Brown Mountain are the unavenged spirits of Belinda and the baby.

Of course, you won't find much scientific evidence lurking around in legends. And scientific evidence is a must for those in the scientific community, a group that's long been interested in the Brown Mountain Lights. There must be a logical, scientifically provable answer to the mysterious lights, they say. After much time and money spent studying them, a variety of theories have been offered.

One says that the lights are caused by a combination of the minerals and gases found on Brown Mountain. Maybe the Brown Mountain Lights are a mirage caused by an atmospheric condition that reflects the lights of nearby towns. OK. But what about the fact that the lights have been seen since the year 1200, way before Ben Franklin's kite and Thomas Edison's brilliance?

The Haunting of North Carolina

In 1913, a U.S. Geological Survey concluded that the lights were actually locomotive headlights from the railroad in Catawba Valley. Three years later, however, a great flood washed out the railroad and no trains ran for months. The Brown Mountain Lights continued to dance up and down the mountain unabated, however. Besides, there's still that year-1200 thing—no locomotives back then either!

A second U.S. Geological Survey then concluded the lights were a result of the spontaneous combustion of swamp gas. Just one little problem...no swamps.

In recent years, a North Carolina paranormal research group has taken an interest in the Brown Mountain Lights. From experiments conducted in their laboratory, they've developed a different hypothesis on the origin of the lights.

According to the group, the lights are most likely a form of plasma, which is the fourth state of matter, and is naturally produced by the mountain. Plasma, they explain, is the product of so much energy being added to a gas that electrons from each atom produce a luminous mass of free-floating electrons and positive ions—resulting in the lights.

Regardless of the cause, the Brown Mountain Lights can be seen on any given night. They're most often seen on clear, moonless nights, but have been seen on foggy, moonlit ones as well. Some of the best viewing sites include the Brown Mountain Overlook on state highway 181, Lost Cover Overlook, on the Blue Ridge Parkway and the Wiseman's View Overlook near Linville Falls.

The Brown Mountain Lights Heritage Festival features exhibits on the various legends surrounding the Brown

Mountain Lights and offers visitors the possibility to see the lights at Wiseman's Point in evening guided tours.

In addition to spotlighting the light mystery, the festival is an opportunity to honor the Wiseman family. Lafayette "Uncle Fate" Wiseman was one of the first to tell the world about the lights. He passed down their story to his great nephew Scotty, a musician who had a 1960s hit about the Brown Mountain Lights. The Heritage Fest also features mountain music, storytelling, and a bonfire, where those who have seen the lights are invited to tell their story at an open mic session.

CAPE HATTERAS LIGHTHOUSE • CAPE HATTERAS

One of North Carolina's most enduring ghost stories is that of Theodosia Burr Alston, the beautiful and gifted daughter of Aaron Burr, one of our country's most powerful and controversial founding fathers.

In 1801, Theodosia married James Alston, a wealthy South Carolina plantation owner, who later became governor of the state. The hot, humid summers took a toll on the native Yankee's health, further damaged by the difficult birth of the couple's son in 1802 and the stress of her duties as first lady.

In 1812 the couple lost their son to malaria, and Burr, worried about his daughter's health and mental state, convinced her to sail to visit him in New York. Alston felt his wife was too frail to make the voyage and, besides, the country was at war with Britain, but she insisted. So, he wrote a letter to the British Navy requesting safe passage for her and on December 30, 1813, put her aboard the schooner the

Patriot for the five or six day voyage. It was the last time she was seen alive.

When the ship had not been heard from by two weeks time, Burr and Alston became frantic. In their search, they found that Theodosia had presented Alston's letter to the British Navy near Cape Hatteras and had received permission to sail on. The soldiers recalled that an especially strong storm blew up not long after the ship headed out. A thorough check from New York to Nassau, Bahamas,

Cape Hatteras is said to be haunted by Theodosia Burr Alston.
Courtesy of NC Tourism.

brought no word of the ship's fate and the two men finally accepted their loss and grieved separately.

Weeks after the disappearance, the citizens of Nags Head, North Carolina, were startled to find a fully-rigged schooner washed up on the beach. The sails were set and the rudder lashed. Everything seemed to be shipshape, except for one thing: it was completely deserted. It was impossible to identify the ship, however, because its name had been painted over.

Despite the fact that the stranded ship was reported, no one seemed to connect the disappearance of the *Patriot* with the sudden appearance of this mystery ship. Years later, a Dr. William Poole treated an Outer Banks woman and was given a portrait as payment for his services. The portrait, he was told, was found aboard the abandoned ship, along with a trunk full of fine silk dresses.

Taken by the beauty of the woman in the portrait, the doctor showed it around, wondering if anyone knew who the lady with fiery hair might be. Finally, he showed it to some friends from South Carolina and they told him it was a portrait of Theodosia Burr Alston, the former first lady of South Carolina.

Still, it wasn't until twenty years later that an article in an Alabama paper finally threw some light on the dark mystery of Theodosia's disappearance. The paper reported that a local man on his deathbed claimed to have been aboard a ship that captured the *Patriot*, murdered all those aboard, and scuttled the ship.

A few years later, there was another deathbed declaration from a fellow pirate. This confession included a bit more detail. The pirate said they had captured the ship off Cape Hatteras and that there was a woman aboard the captured ship, an "Odessa Burr Alston." Intrigued by the lady's beauty, the pirate captain planned to take her captive and make her his woman. When Lady Alston fought him, the pirate told her she could either be his woman or die. She nobly chose death. The dying pirate said he himself had held the plank while the lady, dressed in a flowing white dress, had walked its length and dropped into the cold sea. She had tearfully begged that her father and husband be told of her fate, but obviously, they never were.

Many believe the spirit of Theodosia Burr Alston haunts the beach near the Cape Hatteras Lighthouse. Wearing a long, flowing white dress, she's been seen walking toward Nags Head. She's seen most often during the week between Christmas and New Year's, the time she disappeared so many years ago.

THE FLAMING SHIP • NEW BERN

In 1710, a group of Palatines, a sect of German Protestants, sailed from Europe, bound for North Carolina. They planned to join friends and relatives who were already settled in New Bern.

Knowing the dangers of the high seas, the wealthy families pretended to be poor, only able to afford their passage. Throughout the voyage, they hid their wealth from the captain and crew in hopes of making it to their new home unscathed. It was not to be.

The voyage went well, but it was long and the Palatines were so ready to get off that boat! Finally one afternoon the captain announced they would soon be docking. Eagerly, the Palatines began bringing their belongings from below. In their haste, they allowed some of their riches to be seen by the captain. The unscrupulous sailor devised a plan.

"Sorry, folks," he told them. "It's too late for us to make it into the harbor this evening. We'll have to go first thing in the morning."

Disappointed, but heartened to be so close to the end of their voyage, they once again stowed their belongings and went to bed. When the passengers were sound asleep, the captain and his crew crept from cabin to cabin, brutally massacring each and every passenger.

When they all were dead, the murderers loaded the treasures aboard a life boat and, setting the ship afire, rowed toward shore. Looking back, they saw the deck ablaze. As they watched, the entire ship blazed, burning way past the time that it should have extinguished itself and sunk below the surface.

It continued to blaze and to the pirates' amazement, it suddenly began to move, despite the fact that it was a dead calm night. In horror, they saw it moving at a fast pace straight toward them. Panicking, they rowed as fast as they could, reaching shore and jumping from the boat just as the flaming ship neared shore. The ship sailed back and forth along the beach as the pirates unloaded the boat and divvied up the loot. It was still there when the frightened men took their booty and headed inland, never to be seen again.

The ship burned all night. At daybreak, the flames disappeared, but the ship continued to sail around the bay, every inch charred, but otherwise intact. That night the flames rekindled and the ship once again blazed through the night, then disappeared. Until the next year.

According to legend, every year on the anniversary of the massacre, the blazing ship appears in the waters off New Bern. It sails up and down the beach, disappearing by daylight. It's said this phenomenon will occur until the deaths of the Palatines are avenged.

The Haunting of North Carolina

THE GHOST OF BLACKBEARD • OCRACOKE ISLAND

According to legend, Blackbeard the Pirate is the one who named the Outer Banks' Ocracoke Island. As the story goes, Blackbeard and a large contingent of pirates appropriated the island as a place to party and let their hair down a bit. Locals got wind that the pirates planned to make the island a permanent hideout and decided to put a stop to the whole thing.

Since North Carolina's Governor Charles Eden had thrown his lot in with the pirates, taking a cut of the loot in exchange for his protection, the good citizens took their case to Virginia Governor Alexander Spotswood. The gov'nor commissioned a couple of ships, led by British First Lieutenant Robert Maynard, and dispatched them to break up the pirates' little bash. Bringing back Blackbeard's head on a stake may have been mentioned.

The two ships arrived at Ocracoke on the evening of November 20, 1718. It was a dark night, but Blackbeard knew they were anchored just off the island and he knew they'd come for him. Legend has it that, impatient for the morning and the coming battle, the old pirate cried out "O Crow Cock, O Crow Cock." And, that's how Ocracoke Island got its name.

Well, morning came and Blackbeard and his crew sank one ship straight away. Thinking they'd also killed the crew of the other, they boarded it, unaware the British were playin' possum. A fierce battle ensued. Blackbeard was locked in hand-to-hand combat with Maynard when the Lieutenant drew his gun and shot the pirate square in the chest. To his amazement

Blackbeard kept coming. He shot five more times, hitting his mark each time, but the old buccaneer refused to die.

Seeing Maynard's dilemma, his crew fell upon Blackbeard with their swords, slicing into his body at least twenty times, they later testified. Still, he fought. Finally, Maynard raised his sword and lopped off the pirate's head. Reportedly, Blackbeard's headless torso fell overboard and swam a few laps around the boat before finally sinking. Maynard, wanting proof that the pirate was finally gone, did, indeed, hang his head from the yardarm and sailed back to Virginia.

Since the day Blackbeard lost his head, there have been reports that he haunts, "Teach's Hole," aka Ocracoke Island. It's said his headless body floats on the surface or swims around and around Teach's Hole. There's also "Teach's Light," an unexplained glow that emanates from the shore of Pamlico Sound on Ocracoke. Legend has it that on the nights this light appears, intrepid investigators can hear Blackbeard's ghost tramping back and forth, roaring, "Where's my head?"

In addition to these hauntings, it's also said that in the mist-shrouded dawns of crisp fall mornings, you can see Blackbeard's ship sailing out from Ocracoke Island, in search of new plunder to take.

HAMMOCK HOUSE • BEAUFORT

Hammock House is Beaufort's oldest, and most haunted, house. Built in 1709, it's said to have been built by pirates to use as a landmark to steer safely into the inlet. That's why it was built on a hammock—a small wooded hillock—to make it more visible.

The Haunting of North Carolina

Hammock House has survived both a colorful and a dark history. Of course, you'd expect a house that's almost three hundred years old to have a story or three to tell, but Hammock House seems to have more than its share of tales involving mystery and violent death.

The appearance of the house, however, doesn't hint of the darkness of its past. After years of neglect and abuse, it has been beautifully restored to a close approximation of its original state. But appearances can be deceiving.

Just from the sheer number of deaths known to have occurred here, you have to know there's a ghost or two lurking around Hammock House. One of them is said to be the ghost of Blackbeard the Pirate, who plundered the North Carolina waters in 1718. According to legend, when Blackbeard stayed at Hammock House, he had with him one of his fourteen wives, an eighteen-year-old French beauty he had captured on one of his many raids. Ol' Blackbeard fancied himself a ladies man and considered himself quite irresistible to the opposite sex.

The girl didn't agree. She willfully—and quite vocally—rejected his every advance, screaming and crying so that everyone could hear. Her refusals enraged Blackbeard, who was notorious for his temper. When it came time to head back out to sea, he decided to divorce her—pirate style. Just before leaving, he had her hanged from one of the live oak trees in front of the house and buried her beneath it. It's said that on nights with a full moon, you can hear the poor girl screaming.

The pirate's lady isn't the only spirit hanging around (sorry I couldn't resist). It seems that a beautiful Beaufort woman's seafaring fiancé returned unexpectedly to find her in the arms of another man. Enraged, he threw her down the stairs. She died in a pool of blood on the second floor landing. Some versions of the story say the lover was killed, too. At any rate, blood stains remain today, despite the fact the landing has been sanded and painted many times throughout the years.

The last bit of death and mayhem at Hammock House concerns a story about three missing Union soldiers. It happened on March 23, 1862, when the citizens of Beaufort awoke to find that control of the town had been taken over by Union forces. Seems their officers had noticed Hammock House on their way into town. It was abandoned by this time, and the officers thought it would make a good outpost. So, they dispatched three soldiers to check it out. They were never seen again.

Well, not until 1915, when workmen digging near the back porch discovered the remains of the soldiers and their uniforms. Of course, no one knows how they came to be buried there or who stuck them in their shared grave.

Located just off Front and Fulford streets.

THE HENRY HORACE WILLIAMS HOUSE • CHAPEL HILL

For more than fifty years, Henry Horace Williams was an esteemed and favored professor of philosophy at the University of North Carolina at Chapel Hill. He was part of the Hegelian movement, which was influential in breaking the hold of religious fundamentalism on the country's universities, thereby introducing a climate where a truly scientific philosophy could evolve. At a time when the right to teach Darwin's Theory of Evolution was being divisively debated, Williams's influence prevented the passage of a state anti-evolution law, and he was a major factor in the cultural and intellectual awakening that took place in North Carolina in the early 1900s.

Eccentric, slight of build and bespectacled, Williams was a frugal man, who balked at spending money on unnecessary things—such as indoor plumbing, heat, or telephones. When he first came to the University of North Carolina in 1897, he bought an old farmhouse owned by UNC chemistry professor Benjamin Hedrick.

Built in the 1840s, the house had no toilets, no steam heating, no telephones, not even a bathtub. Throughout the fifty years he lived here, Williams refused to have these conveniences added. Not even his wife, Bertha, could persuade him to spend to renovate their home.

When he died in 1940 at age eighty-two, Williams bequeathed his home to the University of North Carolina, who turned it over to the Preservation Society of Chapel Hill. The house was beautifully renovated in 1972 and now serves as a cultural resource and exhibition space.

Horace Williams is reportedly still sharing his philosophy, perhaps with a group of former students who enjoyed his discourses so much that they've returned to debate through eternity. Williams's thin, bespectacled apparition has been seen in his house—and reportedly has been seen wandering the halls of the ninety-year-old Caldwell Hall, the building that once housed the college's philosophy department. By all accounts, he's a mischievous spirit, often mysteriously moving objects from one room to another.

These events were experienced first-hand by Catherine Berryhill Williams and her sister Jane Berryhill Neblet. The girls, daughters of Walter Reece Berryhill, dean of UNC's school of medicine in the 1940s, lived at the house during their teenage years. Both became acquainted with Williams's spirit soon after moving in and recall incidents of fire utensils being moved. Jane even recalls an instance where a figure appeared at the foot of her bed. When her mother showed her a picture of Horace Williams, Jane immediately identified him as the figure she had seen.

In addition to his mischievousness, Williams would seem to be a fastidious ghost. A caretaker reports that, on occasion, the toilets have flushed by themselves. I'm thinking that's not Horace, however. Bet it's Bertha, who, deprived of the convenience of indoor plumbing in life, is determined to make the most of it in the afterlife!

Located at 610 Rosemary Street.

THE MACO LIGHT • WILMINGTON

One summer night, as the Atlantic Coast train was speeding through the North Carolina darkness, its conductor Joe Baldwin was leaning on the railing of the caboose, smoking and contentedly watching as the darkened landscape sped past. Noticing they were just passing Maco Station, he was surprised to suddenly feel a lurch. Immediately the caboose's speed began to drop. Flipping away the cigarette, he hurried through the caboose to the front platform. Just as he had suspected, somehow the car had come uncoupled. Up ahead, his train was speeding along without him.

Joe knew this was a disaster about to happen. There was a passenger train a few miles behind and it would be only a matter of minutes before it caught up with his rapidly slowing car. Grabbing a lantern, Joe ran back through the caboose and out onto the rear platform. He strained his eyes down the track. At first he saw nothing, but after several minutes he could make out a pinprick of light, still a couple of miles back. In only seconds the light grew larger as the passenger train drew ever closer.

Joe raised his lantern and began waving it back and forth. Maybe the engineer would see it in time to stop. He waved and waved. But the light just kept getting bigger. Soon, he was able to hear the clatter of the fast approaching train. He continued waving the lantern frantically back and forth, back and forth, but the train never slowed. Witnesses said that until the moment of impact, Joe's lantern could be seen waving frantically on the back of the caboose.

The train slammed into the caboose with a terrifying crash of steel on steel. The sound echoed into the night air, reverberating as pieces and parts of train and caboose sailed through the air and scattered for hundreds of feet. According to legend, Joe's lantern landed upright, still lit, amid the wreckage.

For hours, volunteers searched the area for Joe, but it wasn't until morning light that they finally found his mangled body where it had been thrown deep into the woods. They were horrified to find that he had been decapitated. An extensive search for his head was launched but it was never found. Joe was buried, headless, days later.

Not long after Joe's body was laid to rest, his spirit began a restless search for his missing head. People living near or visiting the wooded area around Maco Station began to report sightings of a mysterious light. The sightings occurred at night around the time of the crash. At first witnesses would see a tiny pinprick of light down the track. As they watched, the light, which resembled the light of a lantern, would get larger, as if coming closer, and often it would begin to swing back and forth, beginning to swing wildly as it neared the crash site. After arriving at the crash sight, the light would then move back down the track, getting smaller and smaller until it finally disappeared.

The Maco Light began to appear regularly. It became so frequent, in fact, that engineers approaching Maco would stop their trains, thinking it was a signal. To prevent problems, a new rule was instituted at the Maco Station. Trains were required in this area to use two lights—one red and one green—as their signals. If a single white light was seen, it was to be ignored, for everyone knew it was just Joe out looking for his head again. Or maybe he still felt the need to wave his warning light to help prevent another horrible accident.

People began flocking to the Wilmington area to see the Maco Light and were rarely disappointed. In October 1894, U.S. President Grover Cleveland was traveling through North Carolina when he looked out the window of his Pullman coach and saw a mysterious light waving back and forth—the Maco Light he was told. He even mentioned the sighting in a political campaign speech. In 1924, two local farm boys claimed to have been chased several miles through the woods by the light and during World War II, a soldier home on leave said he also was chased through the woods by a ghostly light.

There was so much publicity surrounding the phenomenon that scientists were dispatched to ascertain a logical explanation. But none was to be found. Maybe it was swamp gas, they suggested. But there are no swamps in the area. A ball of lightning, perhaps. But no storms were going on. And later, some speculated that the Maco Light was just the reflection of automobile headlights. Didn't explain all that activity before the invention of the horseless carriage, however.

In 1977, Atlantic Coast Railroad shut down their line and the tracks were torn up. Since that time, the Maco Light has not been seen. Maybe Joe finally located that missing head. Or maybe, with the tracks now gone, he no longer feels the need to wave a warning lantern. Doesn't really matter. Regardless of the state of Joe Baldwin's spirit, his legend lives on.

THE MORDECAI HOUSE • RALEIGH

The Mordecai House is the oldest residence in Raleigh on its original foundation. Built in 1785, it's named for Moses Mordecai, who married into the Lane family, original owners of this home.

According to legend the house is haunted by Mary Mordecai Turk, who lived in the home for quite some time.

She's been seen numerous times, dressed in Victorian fashion, descending the stairs and entering one of the downstairs front rooms. Unkind remarks about her photograph often result in the photograph being turned over and slammed down. Really. Folks should be more sensitive!

So many stories had circulated about the haunting of the Mordecai house that in October 2003, a North Carolina

The Mordecai House is the oldest residence in Raleigh.
Courtesy of City of Raleigh Parks and Recreation.

paranormal research group, accompanied by Mordecai House staff members and a local television news crew, conducted an investigation there. Hoping for a little supernatural action, the group kicked off the evening with a taped interview of a new Mordecai House staff member who had experienced several recent incidents. Upon reviewing their tapes, the television crew reported capturing a number of "orbs," unexplained balls of light that many believe are evidence of spirits, floating around the staff member throughout the interview. More orbs were seen in the east bedroom.

The Haunting of North Carolina

Later into the evening, a member of the research group was sitting quietly in a chair in the west bedroom—Mary's bedroom—when the chair began to shake, a phenomenon that lasted for several seconds. We're guessing it was Mary's chair and she wanted to have a sit.

In an evaluation of 35 mm photographs taken during the investigation, a photo from the outside into a window of the building showed the appearance of a woman dressed in Victorian fashion. Taken with high speed film, the image appeared complete, like someone was standing at the window.

Observations in a follow up visit to Mordecai House brought the possibility that the image might be a trick of light rather than an actual spirit. But, then, again, maybe not. Perhaps, Mary Willis Mordecai Turk was there, peeking out the window at her visitors with their cameras. She's probably hoping they'll get a good picture of her—to replace that bad one in the front room!

Located at 1 Mimosa St. in the Mordecai Square Historic Park.

Eat, Drink, and Be Merry!

Eating out in Strange But True North Carolina is more than a meal. It's an experience. There are restaurants and bars galore along the back roads trail, some historic, some haunted, some just plain fun.

ALL PEOPLE'S GRILL • DURHAM

Feeling the need for a little blues? Well, spend Saturday night at the All People's Grill, where they serve up a heapin' helpin' of the blues with their Southern country food. APG's been called a chitlin' circuit juke joint, but we checked. There are no chitlin's on the menu. What it is is a down-home, family-run joint, with a country-store kinda feel to it.

The menu may be limited—hamburgers, hot dogs, fried chicken, and fried fish—but the music's not. You'll get your fill of all types of music from blues to jazz to rockin' rock 'n roll. Southpaw guitarist Cool John Ferguson is a local favorite in APG's small band room, where he rips through every music genre as if he were born it. There's also a dance room featuring DJ-spun music just off the band room.

Cool! Blues, Boogie, and Southern comfort food. What more could you ask for?

Located at 6122 Guess Road.

Eat, Drink, and Be Merry!

ANOTHERTHYME • DURHAM

OK. This ain't your meemaw's restaurant. But, while the food might not be your typical Southern fare and the atmosphere might be a tad artsy, it's not pretentious. The restaurant was opened in 1982 by restaurateur Mary Bacon, whose philosophy on food centered around healthy seafood and

Anotherthyme's menu focuses on healthy cuisine.
Courtesy of Durham CVB.

vegetarian dishes, rather than the meat and potatoes that constituted fine dining in the South.

It was an innovative idea back then, this healthy food thing, but Mary Bacon had the secret to selling that idea—her healthy food tasted good. She spent years perfecting her recipes, which fuse the flavors of American, Mediterranean, Asian, and Southwest.

In recent years, she's expanded the menu to include free-range chicken, beef, and pork. And, her portions aren't like most fancy schmancy restaurants, where you wonder who stole your food. You get plenty and you'll be glad you do, for although it's not your meemaw's cooking, it's pretty darn good.

Anotherthyme provides a respite from the hassles of the daily rat race. The building itself, with its exposed brick and trompe l'oeil wall painting is pleasing to the eye and the accompanying music is soothing to the soul.

So pack up Meemaw and come on down!

Located at 109 North Gregson Street.

BACK PORCH RESTAURANT • OCRACOKE

Just like dinner at home on the back porch. OK, so maybe your back porch isn't quite so elegant. And maybe you can't cook like the chef at the Back Porch, but you get the idea.

The food is a favorite of both locals and visitors. Locally-caught, fresh seafood is the emphasis here, and you can get it down-home plain or fancied up with interesting culinary delights, such as Vietnamese lime sauce, pineapple salsa, or balsamic brown butter. Save room for desert though, and don't pass on the bread. It's baked fresh daily.

Open for dinner only at 110 Back Road.

BALI HAI • RALEIGH/DURHAM

OK, what a defunct, stinky cologne's got to do with good food, we don't know (you folks of a certain age know what we're taking about), but, hey, we're game. Good food is about all this little eatery has to offer.

Opened twenty-three years ago, the Raleigh place is a dump. There's no décor to speak of, no menu, and minimum service. That doesn't stop the folks from coming in, though, because the food is that good. And it's not your usual Southern fare. Bali Hai serves up some of the spiciest and the best Mongolian food around.

Eat, Drink, and Be Merry!

You can order your food anywhere from "no burn" all the way to a four-alarm conflagration. It'll raise your heart rate to dangerous levels, open your sinuses, and flash-burn your tongue. Perfect!

Bali Hai recently opened a new location in Durham, which is everything the Raleigh location isn't. It has décor. There's a menu. And there's a modicum of service. Food's the same, though. Good, plenty, and made to order.

Located at 2414 Wake Forest Road in Raleigh; 811 Ninth Street Suite 170 in Durham.

BAR Charlotte • Charlotte

Partaay! That's the cry at BAR Charlotte, where the motto is No Theme, No Attitude, Just Bar. Oh, but, wait! There is a dress code. Don't try to get in wearing sweats or athletic wear and turn that hat back around to the front. They even got a problem with solid colored T-shirts. Go figure.

Anyway, partaay! BAR Charlotte claims to throw the sickest (for all you old folks, that's a good thing) parties around—Mardi Gras, New Year's Eve, and Spring Break all rolled into one. Whew! Sounds like too much work for us old folks. The young'uns like it though.

There's good music, lots of dancing, and the liquor flows. They even got one of those mechanical bulls—now that's something us old folks can remember!

Located at 300 North College Street.

BEAN TRADERS • DURHAM/CHAPEL HILL

We'd like to make fun of this fancy coffee place, but we can't. We like our fancy coffee too much. Of all the hoity-toity trends to wend its way southward, this is the one we like the best.

Anyway, Bean Traders, owned by a young husband and wife team, is a fancy coffee place extraordinaire. They even roast their own beans (twenty-five varieties) right on the spot. Wow. Just the aroma will give you a buzz. And once there, you'll have a hard time deciding from their huge selection, which includes teas, cocoa, root beer floats, frozen coffee drinks, and smoothies. Oh! And don't you dare pass on the pastries.

There are two Durham locations: 249 West State Highway 54 and 714 Ninth Street; the Chapel Hill location is at 116 West Barbee Chapel Road.

BINION'S ROADHOUSE • HENDERSONVILLE

Sometimes nothing will do but a big, thick, juicy steak. For those times, Binion's Roadhouse is the place to go. The place may resemble some of the cookie-cutter chain steakhouses, what with the Western décor and the peanuts served on each table, but Binion's is locally-owned and the service is home-grown friendly. No one's slipped and sued 'em yet, so they encourage you to throw the peanut hulls on the floor. The kids love it.

Located at 1565 Four Seasons Boulevard.

BOGART'S AMERICAN GRILL • RALEIGH

Here's lookin' at you, kid. Bogart's is a 1940s retro kinda place—OK sorta. So, it's big screen TVs with Casablanca showing up there, but what the hey. Actually, retro-chic is how the proprietors describe the décor of their eclectic restaurant. Low lighting and high-backed booths create an intimate atmosphere in which to enjoy your American classic meal—food made from scratch and rotisserie-grilled steaks washed down with classic martinis. Bogie would be proud.

Come early for dinner and stay late to party. There's jazz music playing all through dinner and five dollars gets you into Bogart's Hi5 and Red Room, where you can party with live music or DJ music. You gotta be a night owl, however. The first note's sounded at eleven p.m. and you can dance 'til two.

Located at 510 Glenwood Avenue.

BREAKFAST CLUB • CHARLOTTE

OK, here's the place for you folks not quite of a "certain age" yet. The Breakfast Club (Hey, that was an eighties movie, wasn't it?) is Charlotte's only all-eighties dance club. We're figuring one's enough.

Throw on those leg warmers. Get out those jelly shoes and pointed bras—wear 'em on the outside—and pull that hair up in a side ponytail. Then skip on over to the club, where you can flash dance to the likes of Rick Springfield (what ever happened to him?), Prince, before he was the rock star formerly known as, and Madonna.

After sweatin' to those oldies, you can take a break in the first level lounge with your specialty cocktail with an eighties-themed name, such as "Superfreak" or "Top Gun," and peruse the eighties memorabilia. Oh! Oh! Remember Cyndi Lauper with all that technicolor hair. Ah, the good old days!

Located at 225 North Caldwell Street.

BUTTS ON THE CREEK • MAGGIE VALLEY

Nope. This is not a plumber's convention. They're speaking of pig butts, actually. Roasted pig butts. And they're roasted on hardwood, which gives them that wonderful North Carolina-style smoky flavor. In addition to pig rears, they got cow ribs and catfish, too. The place is rustic, with a porch overlooking Jonathan Creek. Service is good and friendly.

Located at 1484 Soco Road.

CAROLINA INN • CHAPEL HILLS

Want to be served a bit of spooky chill with your fine dining? Then the Carolina Inn is the place for you. Built in 1924, the inn has long played a vital role in the life of Chapel Hill and the University of North Carolina. It was built by UNC graduate John Sprunt Hill, who donated it to the university in 1935 to serve as a "cheerful inn for visitors, a town hall for the state, and a home for the returning sons and daughters of alma mater."

Listed on the National Register of Historic Places, the Carolina Inn is an architecturally significant structure that blends Southern Antebellum style with Georgian and neoclassical features. The original front was modeled after George Washington's Mount Vernon.

The CrossRoads Restaurant, nestled cozily within the inn,

has been described as "a great restaurant that just happens to be in a hotel." The award-winning, four-star cuisine "blends the graceful Southern traditions with progressive American cuisine to create memorable dining experiences."

After dinner, you may want to retire to the restaurant's cozy bar for an after dinner drink. You can sit in one of the sumptuous leather chairs

The Carolina Inn is home to the CrossRoads Restaurant.
Courtesy of the Carolina Inn.

in front of the fireplace and contemplate the ways of the world. If you happen to find a dapper gentleman dressed in the garb of years gone by sitting next to you, don't panic. Just order him a brandy. That's Dr. William Jackocks, the Carolina Inn's resident ghost.

Dr. Jacocks was a physician and a UNC professor who traveled to India to work with the International Health Division of the Rockefeller Foundation. He returned to Chapel Hill in the late 1940s and while he was looking for a home to buy, he stayed at the Inn. However, he liked the inn so much—really, meals and maid service, what's not to like—that he gave up the idea of buying his own place and just stayed on. He lived on the second floor in Suite 252, where he was quite particular about his academic papers and belongings.

Jacock's old suite has been renovated, but staff members suspect he's still there. They report strange feelings and mysterious noises, such as the sound of papers rustling. His favorite prank is to lock guests and staff out of their rooms. So many strange occurrences have been reported that the staff of the hotel asked a local paranormal research group to investigate the inn for ghostly presences. The group's research seemed to confirm that, indeed, there are otherworldly activities taking place at the Carolina Inn. They plan to make further investigations soon.

The inn has been restored, renovated, and renewed. It's got style. It's got grace. And it's got Jackocks, the friendly ghost. What more could you ask for?

Located at 211 Pittsboro Street.

CHEESEBURGER IN PARADISE • ASHEVILLE

This is one of those cheesy (Get it? Cheesy…cheesebur..? Oh, never mind) chain restaurants, but we're big ol' Parrotheads and we just can't resist a taste of the islands. The star of Cheeseburger in Paradise's menu is, of course, the Cheeseburger in Paradise—lettuce, tomato, Heinz 57, onion slice, and a big ol' kosher pickle. Comes with French fried potatoes, but you have to order the cold draught beer. And of course you can get your cheeseburger any way you want it—

even if you want to leave off the big hunk of meat. See, you can substitute a veggie burger in any of the burgers. Naw, thanks.

They also serve stuff like BBQ Jerk Ribs, St. Barts Blackened Chicken, Nawlins BBQ Shrimp, and Shrimp Po' Boy Wrap. Wash it all down with a frozen Buffet-themed concoction, such as the Electric Lizard or the Montserrat Volcano and save room for Some Kind of Sensuous Treat—the wacky chocolate nachos or ummm…key lime pie.

Housed in a weathered beach house, this paradise is the quickest way to escape the daily rat race and sail away to Margaritaville. So drag out the blown-out flops, throw on some baggy shorts, and bone up on the Buffet lyrics. Time to go searchin' for that lost shaker of salt.

Located at 1 Restaurant Court.

CLAWSON'S 1905 RESTAURANT & PUB • BEAUFORT

The building that houses this restaurant played an important role in Beaufort's history. Charles and Mary Clawson were immigrants (Charles was Swedish, Mary was Irish) who founded Clawson's Grocery in 1905 and grew their business into a pub and a bakery. The building dates back to 1870 and housed the canned goods, fresh produce, and the bakery. The Clawson's baked goods became famous throughout Carteret County. Local deliveries were made by carriage—drawn by horses June Bug and Dragonfly.

The building served many businesses throughout the years, but was finally turned into a restaurant and pub in 1977. The proprietors renamed the establishment for its original owners to keep a part of Beaufort's history alive. The current owners emphasize the building's history and help to preserve a bit of days past by displaying memorabilia from the original grocery store.

Clawson's 1905 Restaurant features fine food, such as fresh caught local seafood, steaks, and a variety of pasta dishes. For a taste out of the ordinary, try one of the restaurants dirigibles. Naw, we're not talking about a big ol' helium-filled flying machine. Clawson's dirigibles are giant potatoes stuffed with stuff—seafood, or ham and turkey, bacon, broccoli, red peppers, mushrooms, and such. Save room for dessert. Clawson's homemade mud pie is famous.

Located at 425 Front Street.

DEAN & DELUCA WINE ROOM • CHARLOTTE

All wine, all the time. That's the theme of the Dean & Deluca Wine Room, the only such establishment in Charlotte. Located across the street from the Dean & Deluca's market, which sells wine

Dean & Deluca Wine Room offers more than fifty wines.
Courtesy of Dean & Deluca.

and gourmet food items, the Wine Room offers more than fifty wines in a two-ounce taste, a six-ounce glass, or a "wine flight," a sampler of three wine varieties.

If you don't know a lot about wines, but are interested in learning, this is the place for you. The servers go out of their way to help with your selection without making you feel like a novice. To accompany your wine, you can order cheeses, salads, seafood, and sandwiches.

The bar's atmosphere is elegant, with high ceilings, polished wood, and romantic lighting. A pianist offers light jazz music nightly.

Located at 6822-G Phillips Place Court.

EARLY GIRL EATERY • ASHEVILLE

Traditional Southern fare meets New Age cuisine. That's the hallmark of the Early Girl Eatery, which opened in 2001 and blossomed in popularity as quickly as its namesake—an early-blooming variety of tomato. The restaurant's menu reads like William Faulkner edited by Dr. Andrew Weil.

Take, for example, the biscuits and gravy, where the traditional homemade biscuits are topped with vegetarian herb gravy. How 'bout a grilled cheese? It's pimento cheese grilled with arugula and tomato on wheat. There's even a twist to the cheeseburger. It's farm-raised, hormone-free beef topped with farmstead cheese, basil mayo, lettuce, tomato, and grilled red onions.

Early Girl also serves up traditional dishes, such as barbecue pork roast and a hearty Southern breakfast with two eggs, bacon or sausage, grits, and biscuits. Then there's the blatant

New Age stuff, such as the avocado and sprout sandwich, a vegan bean burger, and the sesame tofu salad.

Another hallmark of the restaurant is its emphasis on using fresh local ingredients. Owners John and Julie Stehling spent much time cultivating a working relationship with local farmers who grow organic produce and free-range, hormone-free meats. Featured in numerous local and national publications, the restaurant has become a favorite with both the young and the health conscious and the traditional Southerners. They have something in common—a love of good food.

Located at 8 Wall Street.

ELMO'S DINER • CARRBORO/DURHAM

Elmo's Diner ain't your typical fifties-era diner. Located in the renovated Carr Mill Mall, the Carrboro location, especially, has an arty flavor to the atmosphere. Yes, there's quiche. And spinach salad. And a hummus platter. But, there's also homestyle roast beef with real mashed potatoes, chicken and dumplin's, and meatloaf.

There's an extensive breakfast menu and you can get it anytime of the day. It's one of the favorite meals. Elmo's is a landmark in North Carolina and a very popular eating place. It's recommended that you come early.

Located at 200 North Greensboro Street, Carrboro; 776 Ninth Street, Durham.

Eat, Drink, and Be Merry!

FROGGY DOG RESTAURANT AND BAR • HATTERAS ISLAND

Feeling froggy? Well, come on over to the Froggy Dog. OK, we admit it, we don't know why this fun restaurant and bar is named for two entirely different species, but we like the name anyway.

The Froggy Dog is open for breakfast, lunch, and dinner, with a full menu for all. They offer hearty breakfasts, an eight-ounce hamburger, and signature crab cakes. Harried parents can drop the kids off in the Tadpole Corner, where the kids can play, while Mom and Dad enjoy a leisurely meal in peace. There's also the Groggy Pirate bar, a staple of Hatteras Island nightlife. And don't forget to stop by Ribbits Gift Shop for a Froggy Dog T-shirt on your way out.

Located at 40050 Highway 12, Avon, Hatteras Island.

GEORGE'S GARAGE • DURHAM

Hey! Can we get an oil change while we wait for our sushi? Naw. But there is live entertainment and dancing! George's strives to be all things to everybody. A popular after-hours hangout, it's a cavernous room, large enough to house a dining room, a buffet line, a full service sushi bar, and an energetic wine bar, complete with a hopping dance floor.

The food is eclectic, ranging from seafood, fresh from George's own boats, to Mediterranean fare to nouvelle cuisine. The buffet line is huge and varied. Its pay-by-the-pound charge makes it a popular spot for lunch.

The place is really jumping on the weekends. Open late, the place offers DJs, music, and dancing into the wee hours. And if you stay past late, not to worry. You can take advantage of the bakery offering muffins, pastries, and biscuits baked fresh every morning!

Located at 737 Ninth Street.

George's Garage is a popular after-hours hangout.
Photo by Jeanna Lee Tahnk.
Courtesy of Durham CVB.

GOOD OL' DAYS RESTAURANT • CHARLOTTE

The fifties feel of Good Ol' Days appeals to young and old(er) alike. There's a nifty retro juke box, and you'll find everything from Belgian waffles with link sausages to deli sandwiches to pizza and burgers on the extensive menu. And of course there are milkshakes. Thick, rich, and creamy ones. So, what if they come in some funky flavors, such as mocha, coffee, and blueberry? They'll still take you back to the Good Ol' Days.

Located at 3351 Pineville Matthews Road.

GROVE PARK INN RESORT AND SPA • ASHEVILLE

The Grove Park Inn, a grand mountain resort that combines old world charm and Southern hospitality, has been

Eat, Drink, and Be Merry!

a favorite of travelers for decades. An architectural wonder constructed at the turn of the century from granite stones mined from Sunset Mountain, it overlooks the Asheville skyline and stuns guests with its breathtaking views of the Blue Ridge Mountains.

You have your choice of dining atmospheres at Grove Park. For world-class cuisine, choose the formal intimacy of the Horizons restaurant. If you're in a more casual mood, there's the Blue Ridge Dining Room and the Sunset Terrace, both of which serve wonderful prime rib. The Spa Café is the smallest and most intimate dining area, and when it's nice, you can choose to sit outside, next to a picturesque waterfall.

A limited menu is available at the Great Hall Bar and Magnolia Lounge. The Great Hall Bar also offers live music and dancing nightly and there's live music available in the wine bar of the Blue Ridge Dining Room. All restaurants come with a breathtaking view at no extra charge.

Also at no extra charge, the Grove Park Inn offers its guests the delicious possibility of an otherwordly experience. You see, the inn is home to the Pink Lady, the spirit of a young woman wearing a pink, frilly dress. According to legend, in the early 1920s, the young woman—wearing a long, flowing pink dress—fell to her death from the inn's fifth floor balcony.

Not long after her death, guests and staff began encountering the apparition of a lady in pink. A friendly sort, she wanders freely around the resort. She's apparently fond of children and is given to playing pranks, such as locking people out of their rooms and turning lights on and off.

Her presence has been caught on film several times. One of the most notable photographs was taken by a guest, who thought he was taking a picture of the inn's beautiful fireplace. When the film was developed, there was a blue, filmy image of a woman standing on one side of the fireplace. The image had not been seen by the photographer when the picture was snapped.

Restaurants at the Grove Park Inn offer breathtaking views.
Courtesy of the Grove Park Inn Resort and Spa.

Before jumping, falling, or being pushed to her death—no one is sure which—the lady in pink was staying in Room 545, and it's here that some of the scary events have occurred. Staff members report hearing a disembodied voice ordering them out of the room and others report the sensation of an electrical presence passing through their bodies.

Today, visitors come from all over the world to stay at the inn with the Pink Lady. They often request Room 545, hoping for an encounter with her spirit. And, she, being a social creature, seems happy to oblige. Hundreds of people have been graced with her presence in the past and appearances are as common as ever.

Located at 290 Macon Avenue.

Eat, Drink, and Be Merry!

HAVE A NICE DAY CAFÉ • CHARLOTTE

If you're one of those folks who thinks the person who came up with that inane seventies phrase oughta be shot, maybe you should go elsewhere. You also might get murderous when you find out this café has no food. But, hey, there's lots of liquor!

This seventies-themed bar is a favored night place, where you can go to relive those days of youth. Ppppuuutt put on your, your, your, your boogie shoes and boogie on down to the non-stop disco music. And if dancing's not your thing, grab a drink and wander around for a looksee. The walls are plastered with seventies memorabilia, from Farrah to Shaun to Marcia. Oh, the days of innocence.

Located at 314 College Street.

LAUGHING SEED CAFÉ • ASHEVILLE

This eclectic little vegan café is one reason Asheville is known as The New Age City. Arty and festive, it has become popular with vegetarians and meatlovers alike. Its name comes from an Indonesian story about a plant with magical seeds. When the seeds were consumed, the consumers became intoxicated with laughter and were able to communicate with the gods.

We carnivores had no idea just how many plants you could eat and just how good they could taste. Nope. Tofu will never take the place of a good, juicy steak, but, hey, it can make a nice barbecue rollup. The Laughing Seed has won numerous awards, including the Best Vegetarian Restaurant in Western North Carolina eight years in a row and has been recognized by such prestigious publications as *Southern Living, Vegetarian Times,* and *The New York Times.*

In addition to the cuisine imbued with an international flair, the restaurant is a soul-soothing oasis in the busy hustle bustle of Asheville, with warm shades, a colorful rainforest mural, and a babbling fountain. There's a bar serving anything from smoothies to martinis and in warm weather, al fresco dining is available on the sheltered patio. Hey, we might could get used to this meatless thing.

Located at 40 Wall Street.

PADDY'S HOLLOW RESTAURANT AND PUB • WILMINGTON

Hankering for a wee bit o' the Irish? Well, drop by Paddy's Restaurant and Pub, known for its low-key atmosphere, good food, fun, and great beer. Take a break from your shopping at the Cotton Exchange and stop in for a pint. Enjoy your favorite sports event on the big screen TV or take a seat out on the Paddy-o, where you can enjoy your food with a view of the Cape Fear River.

Located on the corner of Front Street and Water Street.

PIGGY'S AND HARRY'S • HENDERSONVILLE

Nope. You're wrong. This is not another barbecue joint. It's two restaurants in one. And, it's a wonderful step back in time. A popular eating establishment since the fifties, Piggy's and Harry's is filled with antiques and memorabilia. On one side, you'll find Piggy's, the old-fashioned ice cream parlor, where you can get just about any flavor you can dream up. Harry's has burgers, fries, barbecue, and other goodies.

Located at 102 Duncan Hill Road.

Eat, Drink, and Be Merry!

sMacNally's • Ocracoke

Modesty is not one of these folks' virtues. They not only claim to have the coldest beer on the island, but they also lay claim to Ocracoke's best burgers, and even suggest these culinary delights might be the best in the state. Their food is so good, they say, it will make you want to smack yo' mama. Don't know about you, but my mama would smack me back pretty darn quick!

Modesty aside, Smack's, as it's affectionately known by the locals, is a down-and-dirty raw bar perched on the Anchorage Marina dock. The fishy scents of the sea fill the salty air, while boats sail by, providing a never-ending photograph of island life. The beer is cold, the burgers sublime. Life is good.

Home to Ocracoke's best burgers, sMacNally's is located at Anchorage Marina.
Courtesy of sMacNally's.

If you're craving seafood (It is an island, after all!), you won't be disappointed at Smack's. There are buckets of crawfish to go with the really cold beer, and, of course, you won't want to miss out on the raw oysters, the best little slimy treats nature makes. There's also fried or grilled fish, popcorn shrimp, crab cakes, and steamed clams.

Located at Anchorage Marina.

SMOKEY BONES • CHARLOTTE/FAYETTEVILLE/GREENSBORO/ WILMINGTON

Smokey Bones is a chain restaurant that doesn't know it's a chain. With more than fifty restaurants scattered around the country, you'd think probably the meat was like, prepackaged and shipped. Not so. Their hand-pulled pork and St. Louis-style ribs are cooked over hickory slooowly—for up to eleven hours—so that it's fall-off-the-bone tender and imbued with a rich smoky flavor. It's considered some of the best barbecue ever by some of North Carolina's most discerning palates.

Smokey Bones also serves up some killer burgers and sandwiches. The half-pound Angus or buffalo (yep, it's really buffalo meat) come in specialties, such as the Bleu Portobello and the Smokehouse. There's also a sandwich made with grilled Mahi-Mahi that's been marinated in garlic and is served with a Cajun remoulade and several salad specialties. Kinda makes it hard to choose!

Located at 8760 Jim Keynes Drive, Charlotte; 1891 Skibo Road, Fayetteville; 3302 Highpoint Road, Greensboro; 1055 International Drive, Wilmington.

SPOTTED DOG RESTAURANT • CARRBORO

Not only is the food good, but the menu is fun to read! In keeping with the Spotted Dog theme, the menu offers a plethora of both vegan and meat treats. Order up some Fetchin' Sticks (fried cheese), Diggin' in Hummus, a Kennel Club sandwich, the Field Run salad, or Chicken Chews (chicken strips).

Smokey Bones has more than fifty locations throughout the country.
Courtesy of Smokey Bones.

Opened for several years, the restaurant is one of Carrboro's favorites and locals like to hang out at the bar, which spans the entire restaurant. The restaurant also sponsors local charities through its artwork program. Most of the artwork hanging on the wall has been painted by local women artists and is for sale. Ten percent of each sale is donated to various charities.

Good food. Good atmosphere. Good deeds. So, do as the owners ask. Come. Sit. Stay. Or you can fetch—with some of their takeout.

Located at 111 East Main Street.

SQUIGLEY'S ICE CREAM AND TREATS • CAROLINA BEACH

Wow! Four thousand fifty different flavor combinations. If Squigley's don't got it, it can't be had. In addition to the traditional ice cream flavors, Squigley's will make any flavor combination you request, no matter how weird the request, even, say, a blueberry, peanut butter cup, Oreo. And, they make their own waffle cones!

Located at 208 South Lake Park Boulevard.

SWEET POTATOES • WINSTON-SALEM

Well, shut my mouth! This is Southern cooking with real flair. Right alongside traditional dishes, such as pork chops, fried chicken, and meatloaf, you'll find some that are sure to become traditions. Like barbecued duck, roasted quail, and Carolina Salmon Florentine. In addition, there's a Creole influence, with dishes, such as Gullah Shrimp and Crab Pilau; Catfish Nola, a pan-fried catfish covered with Creole sauce; and a jerk-chicken sandwich called the Voodoo Chicken Sandwich. And everywhere there are sweet potatoes!

There's sweet potato cornbread dressing, sweet potato fries, sweet potato aioli, roasted sweet potatoes, smashed sweet potatoes, and even a build-your-own sweet potato. The desert menu is heavy with the wonderful orange tuber. There's, of course, the traditional sweet potato pie, but that's just the beginning. There's also sweet potato bread pudding and sweet potato cheese cake. Of course, there's also nanner pudding. Oooo and Bourbon Pecan Pie! The restaurant proudly announces that it only uses locally-grown sweet potatoes.

With its bright décor and art-filled walls, featuring local artists, Sweet Potatoes is well-suited to its location in

Winston-Salem's art district. It's a small restaurant and a popular one, so if you're headed out on a Saturday, go early or be prepared for a wait.

Located a 529 North Trade Street.

Tupelo Honey Café • Asheville

"Southern home cookin' with an uptown twist," is how the proprietors of Tupelo Honey Café describe their food. The place has received accolades from all sorts of prestigious food publications. But, we're bettin' there weren't many old Southern tables that served things like fried nut-encrusted brie (it's cheese, y'all) or fried chicken that's breaded with crushed nuts rather than flour. And we're bettin' your mama never made her good old breakfast omelet with havarti, brie, pimento, or, ugh, goat cheese! Well, maybe she should've.

Tupelo Honey, named for the particularly sweet, high-quality honey that comes from special Florida bees, is a New Age—or is that New South?—restaurant. They use only free-range, hormone-free meats and eggs. Many of their dishes are vegan—totally meat and dairy free—and they serve something called "soysage," fake sausage, we're thinking. Imagine, good food that's good for you. It's a totally new concept!

Located at 12 College Street.

Tutto Mundo Lounge • Charlotte

Tutto Mundo is all things to all people, we guess, since the phrase means "everything in the world." Tutto Mundo is one of Charlotte's favored hot spots. Located next door to the upscale Pewter Rose Bistro, the lounge caters to thirty-something professionals, offering solace from a stress-laden day The décor features red velvet draperies, antique leather chairs, and hand- painted murals, striving, it seems, to remind of a New York City loft.

The specialty of the house is that heavenly concoction known as the martooni—uh, martini and with more than fifty vodkas in stock, they can make a mean one! Evenings begin mellow here, allowing time to de-stress. Relax a bit and fill your belly with food from the Pewter Rose's eclectic menu. Chill.

As the night wears on, the tempo picks up as the DJ spins hot music from around the world—part of that "everything" thing, we guess. The energy really gets to hopping and the evening turns festive. Soon the cares of your life are forgotten and you find yourself having fun. Just don't have too much fun. You gotta work tomorrow, remember.

Located at 1820 South Boulevard.

WILSON'S RESTAURANT • WILMINGTON

It's not just a meal. It's an adventure. Wilson's Restaurant is where food meets fun, in thirty-five thousand square feet of food and entertainment. Hungry? Start out in the main dining room, where the chef serves up everything from burgers to Crab Encrusted Salmon. There's a kid's menu, too, with all the favorites, except maybe the fettuccini alfredo. Don't know many kids who'd order that.

Or if you're more interested in the football game than what you're puttin' in your mouth, try out the Sports Bar, where what you're puttin' in your mouth is even better than the game.

Eat, Drink, and Be Merry!

And, boy, can you see the game! The Sports Bar has more TVs than any other bar in town and it has a giant two-hundred-inch big screen, so you can see those guys sweatin' up close and personal like. There's also interactive trivia, live music and entertainment.

For the kids, there's the game room, which has 110 virtual reality games, including a roller coaster simulator, a 1920s-style shootout, and a NASCAR arcade.

Located at 4925 New Centre Drive.

Miscellaneous Miscellany

More points of strangeness on the Strange But True North Carolina trail.

It's The Law!

Better watch your step in our Strange But True North Carolina. You never know when the long arm of the law may reach out and nab you for breaking some of these strange but true laws!

1. It's illegal to sneeze on city streets. I'm sorry, officer. I got a code.
2. It's illegal to use an elephant to plow a cotton field. You just gotta wonder...
3. It's illegal to sing off key. No, really. I'm the next American Idol.
4. In Charlotte, women must have their bodies covered by at least sixteen yards of material at all times. Really.
5. Couples staying in rooms together for one night must stay in rooms with two double beds a minimum of two feet apart. And no making love in the space between the beds, either. Well, you see, I was sleep walking...
6. It's illegal to have sex in a churchyard. Well, duh!

7. It's illegal to sell alcohol at a bingo game. Can't have all those little blue hairs drunk, ya know.
8. It's illegal to be a professional fortuneteller. Of course, I knew you were coming, officer. See? I'm going to brew some tea—with those tea leaves right there.
9. Oral sex is considered a crime against nature. But we wanna know, is it a crime against the state?
10. It's illegal for cats and dogs to fight. But it's OK for them to rain.

Strange Town Names

It's not just the laws in some of our North Carolina towns that are strange. How about some of the town names? Did you know you could travel the globe without ever leaving the state? You could visit Bolivia, Ararat, Turkey, Cairo, Oriental, New Holland, Little Switzerland, Scotland Neck, Dublin, or Emerald Isle. Then there's Dallas, Waco, Scranton, Milwaukee, Gloucester, Broadway, Long Island, and Long Beach.

There are a couple of jewels: Sapphire and Zirconia. So one's a fake. It still sparkles. We've got happy places: Delight, Happy Valley, Joy, Bonnie Doone, and Merry Hill. And peaceful places: Faith and Olive Branch. And, one out of this world place named Orion.

Frogs are big. We've got Frogsboro, Frog Level, and Frog Pond. Then there's Snakebite, Tick Bite, and Lizard Lick. There's a Lower Pig Pen and an Upper Pig Pen. And a Horse Shoe.

OK. Just a few more: Bath, Shacktown, Hicks Crossroads, Meat Camp, Groomtown, Hookerton, Leaksville and New Leaksville, Needmore, Paint Rock, Radical, Climax, Erect, Middlesex, and my favorite of all time: Boogertown.

We don't know how all these towns came by their unusual names (although, we could make a good guess at a few), but following are a few we can tell you about.

AYDEN

Ayden was first known as Ottertown. No, not because it has a plethora of cute little furry creatures running around, but because of the antics of citizen Otter Dennis. Dennis was mean and ruthless and he had so many run-ins with the law that he was finally forced to leave town. Why the good folks felt compelled to name their town after him is beyond us, but seems he set a precedent.

Ottertown, for some reason, appealed to the criminal element. So many misfits banned from other towns settled here, the town became known as "a den" of corruption.

Around 1880, the name was changed to Harrisville, after William Henry Harris, a prominent citizen, who oversaw the move of the town a mile closer to the new railroad and laid out streets.

That name lasted just one year, for when the town applied for a post office, that name was already taken. It was suggested the old name Aden be adopted, adding a y after the A to help dignify the name.

Miscellaneous Miscellany

BANNER ELK

In 1840, a man named Martin Luther Banner was passing through the Elk Creek area of the Blue Ridge Mountains. He was struck by the beauty of the area and declared that one day he would return, a promise he kept. He moved there with his family in 1845 and established the first settlement there in 1848. Within a few years, his extended family had grown to fifty-five. Legend has it that one of those fifty-five members shot the last elk in the area, and that's how the town got its name. For many years it was known as Banner's Elk, and is still called that by some oldtimers.

BAT CAVE

Holy moly, Batman! It's a whole town named for the Bat Cave. Actually, Bat Cave is named for the nearby cave filled with little bats, not one big bat dressed in black plastic.

BOONE

Daniel Boone is most noted for his exploration of the wild Kentucky territory. But he made his mark in North Carolina, too. He moved here with his family when he was eighteen, and it was here that he married Rebecca. In addition to Boone, there's a Booneville, Booneford, Boone's Fork, Boone's Hill, and Boone's Crossroad.

COOLEEMEE

Cooleemee was built as a cotton mill village in 1898 on the shoals of the South Yadkin River. Richard Pearson, a plantation owner in the area, borrowed the name from the Kulami tribe of Creek Indians in Alabama. "Kulami" is said to mean "place where the white oaks grow."

DUCK

This town is named for the huge numbers of waterfowl that once flocked here during the migratory seasons. Maybe. We're bettin' it's also called that for stuff falling from the sky from all those ducks—as in "Incoming! Duck!"

FLAT ROCK

So named for the huge outcrop of granite, said to have been the site of Cherokee gatherings.

FOREST CITY

You're probably thinking this town was named for a beautiful forest nearby. You'd be wrong. It's actually named for a prominent citizen. When first settled in 1877, the town was called Burnt Chimney, for the only portion remaining of the McArthur home. It was renamed in 1887 for citizen Forest Davis.

HATTERAS

Hatteras is named for an area along the Outer Banks that was called "Hatorask" by early settlers.

KILL DEVIL HILLS

The site of man's first flight, this town is steeped in legend.

Miscellaneous Miscellany

Of the many stories about where the name comes from, the most reliable contends it's named for the cases of "Kill Devil Rum" that washed up on shore after a shipwreck during the Revolutionary War.

Kill Devil Hills was the site of the Wright Brothers' first flight.
Courtesy of Tim Hu.

KITTY HAWK

The name of this little town, where Wilber and Orville Wright lived, is reportedly derived from a Native American term for the area. The word originally appeared on English settlers' maps as "Chickehawk" or "Chickahawk" in the early 1700s. By the end of that century, most local residents spelled the name as it is known today, though it occasionally appeared on old deeds with spellings such as "Kittyhuk," or even "Kittyhark."

MAGGIE VALLEY

This beautiful little valley was named for a beautiful blonde-haired, blue-eyed minx. Her father, Jack Setzer, got tired of paying someone five dollars to pick up the remote settlement's mail. He petitioned the U.S. Postal Service to establish a post office in his community. After six months of keeping meticulous records on how much mail was sent and received, his request was granted. The Postal Service requested that he submit a name for the new community. His first few suggestions were rejected because they were already taken. He next submitted the names of his three daughters, Cora, Mettie, and Maggie Mae. Guess you know which one was chosen.

NAGS HEAD

If legends are to be relied upon, this town is named for an ignoble practice conducted by land pirates back in the day. See, many tales were told of the treasures being plundered at sea.

Nags Head was once home to many land pirates.
Courtesy of Nags Head.

The land-bound folks, not having a ship to use, still wanted to get a share of the loot. One enterprising guy came up with an idea. He tied a lantern around the neck of an old horse—a real nag—and led her up and down the dunes known as Jockey Ridge. The light was seen by many a ship's captain at sea. Thinking the light was from a ship at anchor, the captain would sail in, looking to anchor up as well, and would run aground. The ship would then be over run by the land pirates, who made the crew walk the plank, and stole anything of value. They would then torch the ship.

SEVEN DEVILS

There are several legends concerning the name of this town. It might be named for the seven prominent mountain peaks nearby. Or for seven dangerous hairpin curves on the road between Highway 150 and Town Hall. There are the ruins of seven moonshine stills found on the mountain. And, finally, there are the seven devilish sons of a long-forgotten family. Take your pick.

VALLE CRUCIS

"Valley of the Crosses" gets its name because it was once the base for an Episcopal mission in the mid-1800s.

WHYNOT

Seems that at the meeting about what the good folks should name their town, each name was prefaced with "Why not name it..." One tired wag queried, "Why not name it Whynot and let's go home."

Funny Happenings Here

Pig pickin' and possum droppin'. Professional oyster shuckin' and world-class hollerin'. There's just no end to the funny goings on in Strange But True North Carolina.

AYDEN COLLARD FESTIVAL • AYDEN

Ain't nothing' better than a big ol' mess of collards, a huge slice of Southern cornbread, and a slice of raw onion. That's gotta be the reason behind the success of Ayden's annual festival honoring the tasty green treat. Begun more than thirty years ago, it's now a full week of wacky fun.

The Collard Festival kicks off with probably the wackiest events—the Collard Queens Pageant. First is the real pageant, with categories for girls of all age groups. Then comes the "other" pageant—the Collard Blossom Womanless Pageant.

There's live music, dancing, arts and crafts, rides, vendors, a collard cooking contest, and a parade. The highlight is the collard eating contest, where collard lovers can stuff themselves to the puking point. The only rule is that you must eat each pound of collards fully—with anything you want on them. Oh! And you have to keep 'em down long enough to pick up your winnin's! The record so far is eight pounds.

Held the first week in September.

Funny Happenings Here

BLUE RIDGE BARBECUE FESTIVAL • TRYON

In just twelve short years, this festival has become one of the premier barbecue events in the nation. Known around Polk County as "The Barbecue," it draws more than twenty-five thousand pig lovers.

The festival was the brain child of internationally-acclaimed barbecue judge Jim Tabb, whose idea was to combine a world-class barbecue cook-off with lots of fun. Using his connections, Tabb brought in the most experienced judges, which, in turn, drew the world's best barbecuers, which then prompted then-Governor Jim Hunt to designate the event as the official North Carolina State Championship.

In 1999, it was awarded National Barbecue News's National Spirit of Barbecue Award as the best barbecue event in the country. Although the barbecue can be cooked in any form (except microwave), the preferred form by Tar Heels is whole hog, cooked reaaal slow, and eaten picked straight from the bone.

In addition to the world's best barbecue, festival goers are treated to non-stop entertainment—music on two stages, a kid's fun park, and beach bingo. Oh! And don't miss the grape stomping and wine tasting at the nearby vineyard!

Arts and crafts are a big draw for the festival as well. The Foothills Craft Fair is not your everyday craft show. This juried fair features exhibitions from the nation's top artisans in all types of media, including oils, acrylics, watercolors, mixed media, photography, and sculpture.

The event is held at Harmon Field at the foot of Warrior

Mountain and on the banks of the Pacolet River. In one of North Carolina's most beautiful settings, you can have your fun and eat your pig in comfort, despite the summer heat. There's a local geographic phenomenon known as the "isothermal effect," which keeps the area a good ten degrees cooler than surrounding areas.

This is a pig pickin' you won't want to miss.

BLUE RIDGE WINE FESTIVAL • BLOWING ROCK

At what other festival can you become an exalted member of the Order of the Purple Toe? None other, we say. None but this one, where you can join in the grape stomping, which used to be the main method of wine making. Now it's just good, sloppy fun.

Not only that, but also at the Blue Ridge Wine Festival, which honors North Carolina wines, you can sample the featured vinos, enter your wine in the winemaking contest, help judge the Fire on the Rock, a cook-off between the city's best chefs, join in the dancing at the Stomper's Ball, and enjoy five-star dining at area restaurants. There's also kid's activities and plenty of live music.

Held the second week in April.

BROWN MOUNTAIN LIGHTS HERITAGE FEST • LINVILLE FALLS

The Brown Mountain Lights are North Carolina's most abiding mystery. The glowing balls of red, orange, green, and blue move around Brown Mountain in unpredictable patterns and have been visible for hundreds of years. Numerous important studies have been conducted on the phenomenon, but still scientists are stumped for an answer to their origin. The lights were featured in the 1940 novel *Kill One, Kill Two* by W. Anderson and in an episode of the television series *The X-Files*.

At the Linville Falls location, you can even get in on a party celebrating the lights.

BREWGRASS FESTIVAL • ASHEVILLE

The Brewgrass Festival combines two essential North Carolina staples: cold beer and hot bluegrass. It showcases local craft breweries—Asheville alone has four—and some small out-of-state breweries. Visitors have the opportunity to sample more than one hundred different beers, including perhaps the most unusual: blueberry. Guess that's to go with the Bluegrass.

National and regional musicians provide entertainment and there's plenty of food to use as an excuse to drink beer—gotta wash it down, ya know!

An added bonus is that all proceeds go to benefit the Western North Carolina Big Brothers/Big Sisters program. So, go. Eat. Drink. And remember, it's all for a good cause.

Held annually in September.

BUGFEST • RALEIGH

This festival bugs us. It's really fly! Yeah, sorry. Anyway, as one of the nation's largest single-day bug events, the North Carolina Museum of Natural Sciences' Bugfest is filled with buggy fun for the unsqueamish of all ages. Through educational and entertaining displays, exhibits and activities, you'll learn all about the pests of the world, including insects, arachnids, and anthropods.

You just won't believe some of the special events planned. See the amazing Beebearding, where a local beekeeper "grows" a beard of bees, a demonstration that helps understanding of the queen bee and her hive. And you won't want to miss the Roachingham 500 roach race, with the souped up (maybe with Campbell's Tomato) roaches. Roachard Petty is the returning champ.

Kids, no doubt, will love every minute of the creepy-crawly presentations, such as Bugs in our Beds, Ants in our Pants: The Buzz on Bugs!, and What Makes Insects Tick? They also can get their favorite bug tattooed somewhere (temporary) and participate in building a robotic bug.

Grownups will love the CSI Traveling Exhibit and the Forensic Entomology: Using Science to Solve Crimes.

Beebearding is one of the demonstrations you'll find at Bugfest.
Courtesy of NC Museum of Natural Sciences.

If you're brave, visit the Café Insecta. This is where the Bugfest demonstrates just how tasty some creepy crawlers can be. Try out such menu items as Gazpacho with krill.

Funny Happenings Here

It's a fun-filled, bug-packed day. There is one irony, however. After spending so many hours up close and personal with all the little buggies, you may get to feeling warm and fuzzy about 'em. That's when you learn the Bugfest is sponsored by Terminix of Eastern North Carolina!

BURLINGTON CAROUSEL FESTIVAL • BURLINGTON

Well, here's one that'll have you going around in circles all day. The purpose of the Burlington Carousel Festival is to raise funds for the Carousel Restoration Fund, which is used for the upkeep and care of Burlington City Park's antique carousel.

The carousel is a three-row menagerie carousel, built around 1910 by the Dentzel

The Burlington Caousel was built around 1910.
Courtesy of Burlington Recreation & Parks.

family, the world's premier carousel makers. Only two dozen of the many carousels made by the family between 1837, when they immigrated to the U.S., and 1924, remain. Burlington's was bought in 1948 from Carl Utoff the owner of Forest Park Amusement Park in Genoa, Ohio, who had bought it in 1924.

Built during the "Golden Era" for carousels, Burlington's carousel has forty-six hand-carved wooden animals. Noted for their realism, the Dentzel carvers included veins and muscles on their animals. Eyes are glass with pupils and the tails are made of real horse hair.

The Burlington Carousel Festival has been recognized by the governor of North Carolina as one of the state's best festivals and by Travelocity as one of the ten top local finds in North Carolina. In 2005, more than thirty thousand people attended.

The festival features national entertainers on its main stage and there's plenty of music and entertainment and food throughout the weekend. A children's area includes the opportunity to ride on Burlington's treasure—the Burlington Carousel—and other park rides. The Artist Alley features more than ninety fine artists and craftsmen, many of whom specialize in carousel artwork, exhibiting their work. So, come make the rounds!

Held the third weekend in September.

CROAKER FESTIVAL • ORIENTAL

Don't croak. But this is a croaker of a festival. And we ain't talking frogs. But it does sound kinda like one. Actually, for you landlubbers, the Atlantic croaker is a fish. It gets its name from the unusual drumming sound it makes by vibrating its swim bladder with special muscles.

Every July, the town of Oriental celebrates the very vocal, very tasty little fish with a wacky festival. There's a croaker parade. But folks are real picky about their floats in this parade.

Funny Happenings Here

Just grab something—a wheelbarrow and a friend, maybe. Hey, grab a garbage can and roll it in front of you. Any old thing will do. The object here is just to have fun.

There are Croakette and Croaker Queen Pageants, live entertainment, boat races, food, baking contests, and dancing in the streets. And since it's held on the Fourth of July weekend, the festival concludes with a croaked-out fireworks display.

DILLSBORO LIGHTS AND LUMINAIRE • DILLSBORO

Every December, this tiny village lights up, literally. The town itself is an enigma. Despite a population of just two-hundred, Dillsboro sports more than fifty shops, galleries, restaurants, and inns and is known for all manner of arts and crafts.

Every year, the buildings of the town are decorated with traditional luminaries—small white paper bags with candles in them—and are decorated with greenery and thousands of white lights. The shops, restaurants, and inns are open to the public, with treats offered. The event serves as the town's Christmas party, with Santa visiting at night and the Santa Express train chugging in and out of town. There's entertainment as well, with Highland dancers and traditional acoustic music, including bagpipe bands, brass ensembles, and children's choirs.

Held the first two Fridays and Saturdays in December.

FARMER'S DAY • ROBBINS

You know how an idea can just snowball? Well, that's what happened in Robbins in 1955, when Robbins resident Curtis

Hussey and two of his cousins were granted permission to have an annual Robbins Farmer's Day Parade. Curtis became the Wagonmaster for the parade, riding in his 1906 covered wagon that his wife, Beulah, made a new cover for every year.

By 1958, the idea was catching on, with sixty-five entries, and a two-dollar prize for the best wagon. Ten years later, there were three hundred entries and four hundred in ten more. In 1994, Curtis's son Odell took over as Wagonmaster, and still the festival grew.

In 2001, Curtis's Farmer's Day Festival was chosen as one of Southeast Tourism's Top Twenty Events and in 2005, more than thirty thousand people attended. There's almost too much to do. There's a rodeo, arts and crafts, a pottery auction, food booths, pony rides, carnival rides, fireworks, a performance by the Green Beret Parachute Team, all kinds of music, dancing, a Mule Show, and border collie herding demonstrations. The Robbins Farmer's Day Parade is held on Saturday morning and on Saturday afternoon there's the Parade of Tractors, featuring antique tractors and lawn mowers. Geez! What more could you want?

Held the first weekend in August.

FESTIVAL OF THE ENO • DURHAM

In 1965, the proposed flooding of the Eno River Basin prompted the formation of the Eno River Association, a group dedicated to preserving the basin and all its natural treasures. It was through their efforts that the Eno River Basin was admitted into the state park system in 1973.

Funny Happenings Here

To help preserve the area and to continue to add acreage to the park, the association held its first Festival of the Eno in 1979. In the ensuing years, the festival has become one of the state's

The Festival of the Eno helps raise money to preserve the Eno River Basin. Courtesy of Durham CVB.

premier events. Each year, more than thirty thousand people attend the festivities, held on the banks of the beautiful Eno River.

One of the most important features of the festival is its award-winning "Trash free" recycling program. Through a collaborative effort between organizers, vendors, volunteers, and participants, a monumental effort is made to minimize the waste generated and to recycle or compost as many materials as possible. Since institution of this policy in 1992, the festival has reduced the amount of trash produced by 90 percent.

Held annually on the Fourth of July weekend.

FIRE ON THE MOUNTAIN • SPRUCE PINE

Slow down! The mountain isn't on fire. The fire's all contained in the blacksmithing pits in this white-hot festival, which celebrates blacksmithing, a proud tradition in Spruce Pine. Blacksmithing's importance to the community dates back to the days of Daniel Boone. During the thirties and forties, Spruce Pine became a center of blacksmithing, when the Boone brothers, descendents of the famous pioneer, established a base of operations here.

Blacksmiths were the engineers of their day, fashioning tools and functional items for home and farm. Their products included plows and wagon wheels, kitchen knives and hearth axes.

The availability of agricultural equipment and automobiles during the nineteenth century sent blacksmithing into decline.

Fire on the Mountain is an annual blacksmithing festival. Courtesy of Spruce Pine Main Street.

Not in Spruce Pine, however. Daniel Boone VI and brother Lawrence brought national attention to the town when they were commissioned to produce the reproduction iron for Colonial Williamsburg, the restoration of Williamsburg, Virginia. The huge project helped to infuse Spruce Pine with prosperity and a sense of purpose.

Funny Happenings Here

Today, blacksmithing has experienced an upswing, with blacksmiths now becoming "artists" producing sculpture and functional artwork, such as towel bars and other household items. Fire on the Mountain attracted blacksmiths from all over the Southeast, including Daniel Boone VII, a blacksmith who operates the historic Boone Forge in Virginia.

Held annually in April.

GOURD FESTIVAL • RALEIGH

Geez! It's an engorgement of gourds. There are gourd animals, gourd Christmas ornaments, gourd bowls, gourd baskets, gourd purses, gourd hats, gourd toys, gourd dolls, gourd jewelry. There's the biggest gourd. The smallest gourd. Historic gourds. Exotic gourds. Whew. You get the picture.

The annual Gourd Festival brings together gourd lovers from all over the country to pay homage to this innocuous cousin to the squash. There are eighty different competitions for gourd artwork. You can meet

The Gourd Festival has eighty different competitions for gourd artwork.
Courtesy of North Carolina Gourd Society.

gourd craftsmen and learn how they turn the vegetable into objects of lasting beauty. Learn how to grow them. Prefer the simple route? No problem. All manner of gourd artwork is on sale. There's also music, food, and fun.

Held annually in September.

LAZY DAZE ARTS & CRAFTS FESTIVAL • CARY

This one's mis-named. OK, so it's held during the lazy, hazy days of summer, but, by golly, there's so much to see and do packed into the two days of this lively street festival that there's no way they can be called "lazy days."

In the last thirty years, the Lazy Daze Arts and Crafts Festival has become one of the South's top festivals, drawing in more than fifty thousand people every year. More than four hundred artists fill the area with their artwork. There's lots of music and lots of food—including a delicious pancake breakfast—and plenty to do.

Held the fourth Saturday in August.

LEXINGTON BARBECUE FESTIVAL • LEXINGTON

As the official Barbecue Capital of the World, Lexington is expected to have North Carolina's premier barbecue festival and it doesn't disappoint. In fact, the town and the whole of Davidson County go whole hog. They've even declared the entire month of October as Barbecue Month, with a herd of exciting events occurring throughout the month. There's the Tour de Pig—the annual cycling event that benefits Davidson County's Mental Health Association. There's golf and tennis tournaments, the Hawg Run, and the Barbecue Cheer Off, all of which involve some of the Southeast's top athletes.

All these activities culminate in the Lexington Barbecue Festival, held one of the two last Saturdays in October. And what a festival it is. Its first year, 1984, the festival drew more than thirty thousand barbecue lovers and saw more than three thousand pounds of pig consumed. By 1994, the numbers had swelled to more than one hundred thousand people and eleven thousand pounds of pig. The festival had become so popular that the city proposed a radical idea to the state pork producers association: Why not hold the annual North Carolina Championship Cook Off in Lexington?

Since that time, the Lexington Barbecue Festival has continued to grow—in numbers of people and in numbers of attractions, most of them pig related.

There's the Chop Shop and Lumberjack Show, the Hogway Speedway Racing Pigs, and not to mention brewing of the Fine Swine Wine. And much, much more!

MAYBERRY DAYS • MOUNT AIRY

Did we mention Mount Airy is Andy Griffith's home town? Every year the town, in conjunction with the Surry Arts Council, holds a three-day festival to celebrate its connection with this American icon.

The Mayberry Days festival is a step into a parallel universe, where Barney still patrols with a lone bullet in his pocket. You can stroll down Main Street to Floyd's Barbershop, where the sign proclaims "Two Chairs—No Waiting" and owner Russell

Hiatt has been cutting hair for more than fifty years. After your ears have been lowered , you can amble on over to Wally's Service Station, open since 1937 (OK, so there's gourmet basket service there now, but that's just details). Then mosey over to the Snappy Lunch diner, where you'd expect to see Barney spoonin' with Thelma in a back booth. After that, drop into the Old Mayberry Jail, where we all spent so many hours with Andy and Barney. The patrol car's parked right out front, and if it's Sunday morning you may even find ol' Otis passed out in his cell. Wake him up and send him home to his long-suffering wife. Time to get ready for church.

Festivities for Mayberry Days the Mayberry Days Parade, Colonel Tim's Talent time, and Mayberry trivia. Throughout the weekend you'll see well-known Mayberry citizens—both real and look-alikes—mingled in the crowd.

Held the last weekend in September.

NATIONAL HOLLERIN' CONTEST • SPIVEY'S CORNER

If you grew up in the country, you know that hollerin' was serious bidness. If you wanted to be heard, in an emergency, to call someone in from the fields, or just to pass the time, by golly, you had to holler. So developing a good, loud, attention-getting yell was a vital part of growing up in the rural South.

Back in 1969, the folks of Spivey Corners needed a way to raise money for their volunteer fire department. What better way than to stage a hollerin' contest? It was a skill most folks in the area still possessed at the time. So, the publicity went out, and little Spivey Corners, population forty-eight, was inundated with contestants and observers.

Funny Happenings Here

The contest has been held every year since then and Spivey Corners has hollered its way into international attention. Every year, hollerers from all over the world show up in Spivey Corners to scream their guts out for fun and prizes.

There are five ear-splitting contests: the Whistlin' Contest, the Conch Shell Blowin' Contest, the Fox Horn Blowin' Contest, the Junior Hollerin' Contest, the Ladies Callin' Contest (the ladies "called" their husbands in from the fields), and the big daddy of them all, the National Hollerin' Contest.

Held annually in June.

NEW YEAR'S EVE POSSUM DROP • BRASSTOWN

We love this one! It all started in 1990 with a chance remark to Clay Logan, owner of Brasstown's only gas station. It was a few days before New Year's Eve and someone remarked that if New York had their glass ball to drop, why couldn't Brasstown drop a possum? "Hmm…" thought Logan. Indeed, why not?

So, he caught one of the furry little carrion eaters, fashioned a plexiglass cage for it, and ran it up to the roof of his gas station. He passed the word around town, and, so in front of a crowd of thirty, he counted down to midnight, and lowered the discombobulated marsupial by rope to the ground, ending with the words, "The possum has landed!"

Well, the Possum Drop was a popular event in little Brasstown and Logan decided to make it a yearly thing. The Possum Drop has now evolved into a full-fledged New Year's Eve bash—and the dropping of the possum at midnight is the least wacky occurrence. There are fireworks and musket ball firing, live music, homemade cider all around, food, and the wackiest event yet—the Miss Possum Pageant, where big, hairy guys in dresses and stilettos vie for the title.

Brasstown and Logan have worked hard to cash in on the fame of the Possum Drop. Logan's gas station now sells all sorts of possum merchandise, such as stuffed possums, Possum Drop T-shirts, coffee mugs, and canned possum. He's dubbed the town The Possum Capital of the World.

Held annually on New Year's Eve.

Residents of Brasstown drop a possum every New Year's Eve.
Courtesy of Clay's Corner.

NORTH CAROLINA OYSTER FESTIVAL • SHALLOTTE

Every year, the Brunswick Islands celebrate the oyster and its benefit to their economy by serving up more than two hundred fifty bushels of them to more than thirty thousand people. If you don't like 'em raw, don't despair. You can get them fixed any way you want—fried, steamed, baked, broiled, and even stewed up in a delicious, creamy oyster stew.

The big event of the Oyster Festival is the Oyster Shucking Contest, with amateur and professional divisions. You probably are thinking, oh, fun. But you'll be surprised just how exciting oyster shucking can be. And it has to be done just right, too. Shuckers receive penalties for damaging the oysters during shucking. Winners of the professional contest go to the National Oyster Shucking Championship in Maryland and may advance to the World Oyster Shucking Championship in Ireland. Who knew?!

Held the third weekend in October.

Ramp Convention • Waynesville

Seventy-three years celebrating ramps? Really, what's to do, roll up and down them? Oh, hang on. Not that kind of ramp.

For the uninitiated, the ramp is an onion-like vegetable that was a common spring staple in the Appalachian region. The wild-growing plant tastes like an onion with a bit of garlic thrown in, and back in the olden days it was believed to have healing powers. There's just the one thing: The plant's odor is so pungent that it'll make your dog sneeze and your cat run away.

Despite that one little drawback, the folks of Western North Carolina have been celebrating this reeking little vegetable since the 1920s. Today the Ramp Festival is much the same as it was back then, filled with bountiful food, music, dancing, politicians, and, the highlight, the crowning of the Ramp King and Queen.

Come join the fun. Just don't forget the breath mints!

Held annually in May.

SONKER FESTIVAL • MOUNT AIRY

Unless you were raised in North Carolina, you probably have no idea just what a sonker is. No doubt you've eaten sonkers, you just didn't know it at the time. See, a sonker is a deep-dish berry pie or a berry cobbler, with one difference. There's more berries in a sonker than in your everyday, ordinary cobbler.

Traditionally, sonkers were desserts made using whatever was on hand. Usually made from berries, they also could be made from sweet potatoes. The traditional sonker usually was big — made to feed a multitude, such as, say a group of farmhands.

The Sonker Festival is held at the Edwards-Franklin Home.
Photo by Robert Merritt.
Courtesy of Surry County Historical Society.

Every fall, Mount Airy celebrates that sonker with a festival. Held at the historic Edwards-Franklin home, built in 1799, the festival features old-time string music, dancing, and sonkers.

Held in October.

Funny Happenings Here

WATERMELON FESTIVAL • FAIR BLUFF

The North Carolina Watermelon Festival got its start with the rivalry between two neighboring farmers, A.J. Worley and Monroe Enzor Sr. Beginning in 1979, the two friends started growing watermelons and each year they would cart their watermelons to the town of Fair Bluff and weigh them. The one with the biggest watermelon got braggin' rights for the year.

With each passing year, excitement in the town over the rivalry grew. Legend has it that the two began hiding their watermelon patches to keep their prize fruits from being stolen. Each year, they would chuckle over the notching stick they both claimed to keep, though the existence of the sticks was never proved. It's said that in some years, the two would switch melons, depending upon which they had decided would walk away with the glory that year.

As the crowds grew for the watermelon weigh-in, the friends started the Fair Bluff Watermelon Growers Association, Inc. and decided to sponsor a festival. The first one was held in 1985 and it soon became an annual event. The two friends died within a week of each other in 1991, but their spirits are still felt by the old timers who remember their rivalry with affection.

Held in July.

WOOLLY WORM FESTIVAL • BANNER ELK

Forget Punxsutawney Phil. We're off to the Woolly Worm Waces! How much more Strange But True can you get? See, for generations the residents of the High Country have known of the particular weather forecasting skills for the black and brown woolly worm. They've studied the worm and believe that the thirteen brown and black segments of the woolly bear worm correspond to the thirteen weeks of winter. The lighter brown a segment, the milder that week of winter and the darker black a segment, the colder and snowier that

The Woolly Worm Festival is held in October.
Photo by Jim Morton.

week will be. Ah, but all worms are different. So, which one should be the lucky worm used to forecast the coming of Spring? Hey! Let's race 'em! The winner will be this year's weather worm!

So, since 1978, the good folks of Banner Elk have sponsored the Woolly Worm Festival, officially sanctioned as the deciding factor in the woolly worm winter predictor. So how do you race a worm? Well, you tie three-foot lengths of string where they hang down. Contestants choose their worms and give them colorful names, such as Merryweather, Patsy Climb, and Dale Wormhardt. They then place their worms on a string and start urging them on. The first worm to reach the top of his string wins that heat.

Funny Happenings Here

The races begin around ten in the morning. Each heat has around twenty contestants and the heats last until around 4:00 p.m., when the final race is run. The winner of that final race gets one thousand dollars in prize money, and his worm is designated as that year's official weather worm.

Held the third weekend in October.

Strange But True Culture

Artists, world-class storytellers, music, and music men—it's culture with a twist in Strange But True North Carolina.

Artists

Folk Artists. Self-Taught Artists. Outsiders. Whatever you call them, it's been said that there's just one rule in folk art: The artist must be as interesting as his art. That's not a problem here!

RICHARD BROWN

Born in Littleton in 1960, Richard Brown graduated high school and attended Halifax Community College. A man of promise. The promise went awry, however, when Brown became the "town drunk."

These were hard years and Brown continued to drink himself into oblivion to the point that his stomach was dangerously ulcerated and he had regular DT episodes. It took a near-death experience—in the form of a two-day/two-night seizure—to finally turn him around. During that time, he experienced the classic into-the-light phenomenon, with his dead sister beside him telling him "It'll be alright." Surviving the experience, he later testified in church and begged God to take away his seizures. From then on, he never drank or used profanity.

It wasn't until his mother became ill that he began a foray into art, making unusual sculptures to take his mind off his mother's suffering. His sculptures are of a military nature. Although he was never in the military, he says his years as the town drunk made him feel as if he'd been through a war.

Using such materials as wire, Styrofoam, and spray paint, he constructed such things as his Tower Louise 2000, an eighty-four inch high, twenty-eight inch wide tower made of Styrofoam, hot glue, glitter, and wire. Models of aircraft carriers and other military ships hang Christmas tree-like from the tower. Brown says all of his sculptures are named for his mother, Louise, because she is his inspiration.

Today, Brown is a successful businessman. His shop, Brown's Flower Shop, on Main Street in Littleton is filled with his sculptures as well as his artistic flower arrangements.

MINNIE EVANS

Born in a log cabin in Pender County, Minnie Evans is perhaps the best known North Carolina outsider artist. As is the norm for outsider artists, she came to art later in life. She was in her early fifties, when a voice told her to "draw or die."

Evans said she had experienced visions beginning in childhood and it was these visions the voice had ordered her to draw, which she began to do in 1935. First working in ink and graphite, she began drawing on small pieces of paper while at work at Airlie, a perfect Eden-type setting.

Her visions were biblically inspired and so, too, her artwork. She is known for these religious renderings, including totem-like landscapes of plants, animals, eyes, people, and angels all blended together. In the 1940s, she began using crayons, in addition to ink and pencil, and later added oil to her repertoire. Her paintings are brightly colored and show an influence of Indian, Tibetan, African, and other cultures, despite the fact that she had no formal art training.

"My whole life has been dreams...sometimes day visions. They would take advantage of me. No one taught me to paint. It came to me," she said.

JAMES HAROLD JENNINGS

James Harold Jennings, shy and reclusive as a child, was home-schooled by his school teacher mother in their home in Pinnacle. Jennings lived with his mother her until her death in 1974, at which time he moved out of the home where he'd grown up and moved into a set of school buses he had assembled across the road. It was at this time that his creative forces were awakened.

Working from daylight until dark everyday, he began assembling painstakingly detailed wooden sculptures. He made everything by hand because he chose to live without electricity. By the time of his death by suicide in 1999, he had constructed more than four thousand sculptures.

Jennings's inspiration came from many contemporary sources, such as *National Geographic*, comic books, and tabloids. He's famous for his many action-filled fight scenes and for his humorous works. He imbued his work with elements of his personal philosophy, influenced by spirituality, astrology, and the occult. Some of his works, such as his Amazon Women painting, hint at a belief in the superiority of women over men.

By 1985, his yard in Pinnacle had become a fanciful roadside attraction, filled with his vividly colored sculptures, working Ferris wheels, whirligigs, and spectacular crowns. Although he remained shy, he welcomed art lovers from all over the world to tour his home gallery.

CLYDE JONES

Many of us let the hard times slice us to ribbons like a knife, laying open our souls like a bleeding wound. Others of us, take that knife and carve the hard times into art that touches the soul. Clyde Jones is the latter. He, in fact, uses the very instrument that brought on his hard times to fashion his art.

Jones, born in Bynum in 1938, was a laborer and a logger at a local mill until 1979, when he severely injured himself with a

Clyde Jones has filled his yard with hundreds of his carvings.
Courtesy of Jackie Helvey.

chainsaw. While recuperating from the disabling injury, he took up the chain saw and began cutting and assembling roots, stumps, and pieces of wood into animal sculptures.

Jones has filled his yard with hundreds of these carved animals, adding more and more each year. He calls his place The Haw River Critter Crossing. It's a whimsical place, with practically every inch of the yard covered with his creatures. His house, too, is fanciful, painted sky blue with animals, such as dolphins, dinosaurs, whales, and turtles.

Guess Jones ran out of room before he was ready to stop creating, for the entire village of Bynam also sports his sculptures. There are Jones's dog critters protecting homes, peeking out from bushes, and adorning the streets. In the local playground, a tree that reportedly fell during a hurricane has been transformed into a large, brightly painted gator.

Jones has won many awards for his critters and, in addition to the locals who make regular trips, celebrities such as Mikhail Baryshnikov have visited his Critter Crossing. He's so well-known and appreciated in Bynam, that the town recently held Clydefest, a festival in his honor.

Despite its popularity, Jones refuses to sell his work, preferring instead to donate it for fund raising, or sometimes to give away to a child. He loves children, he says. Of all the enjoyable aspects of becoming an artist, he says, having the opportunity to teach art to children is his favorite.

Strange But True Culture

VOLLIS SIMPSON

A Chinese proverb says, "When the winds of change blow, some people build walls and others build windmills."

Vollis Simpson is one of those windmill kinda guys. Born in 1919, he had been a machine repairman who had worked hard for all of his years, but the winds of change were blowing into his life. It was 1985, and he was getting on up in years. Time to retire, to sit back, and relax. But Simpson soon learned that sitting back and relaxing was not his forte. He needed something to do. So, he began tilting at windmills.

Well, actually he started building them. It was something he already had experience in. Back during World War II, when he was stationed in the Philippines, he had built a windmill-powered washing machine for his unit. After he returned home he built a large windmill that powered a heating system in his house.

Gathering up discarded industrial products, he began assembling whirligigs—windmills that are just for show. He used anything and everything as materials and painted the finished products in bright, cheery colors. When the wind blew and the whirligig wheels turned, these masterpieces of engineering danced or spun or fluttered. And they sang a chorus of beautiful wind music.

Before long Simpson's farm was a wonderland of sight and movement and sound. Even at nighttime. Especially at nighttime. For Simpson had covered his work with reflectors, so the headlights of passing cars would turn the darkened farm into a carnival scene.

News of his wondrous whirling wind machines got around and people began to come out for a looksee. Requests began pouring in and Simpson began filling them, making small whirligigs for homes and yards and sometimes large ones. He was selling them for up to a thousand dollars each. Soon, folk art experts took notice and Simpson was declared a genius. He was commissioned to create whirligigs for the High Museum of Art in Atlanta, Georgia, the North Carolina Museum of Art, and the American Visionary Art Museum in Baltimore, Maryland. In 1996, he was commissioned to create four pieces for the Summer Olympics in Georgia. The pieces, a man sawing, a duck, a water-pumper, and a man on a unicycle, were placed in downtown Atlanta.

Simpson is still making his whirligigs and people still come from all over the world to see his whirligig farm. It's truly a wonder to behold—and to hear. So if you're any where near Lucama, don't miss the opportunity to stop by. Who knows? You might be lucky enough to catch the windmill man at work.

Music From the Heart

Southern Appalachia is a complete jumble of heritages, most of which arrived from across the Atlantic more than two hundred years ago. Because the mountains isolated Southern Appalachian settlements from other people and groups, the traditions they brought remained virtually unchanged for centuries.

Balads, which recorded and preserved history, were sung by women and accompanied by men on fiddles and banjos. Mass production of instruments soon made the music more available to the parlors and porches of North Carolina.

Another big influence was the radio. The first radio station to broadcast to the mountains was Asheville's WWNC. Soon, local artists were heard playing on the radio, with the most popular show being *The Farm Hour.* Because they were able to "advertise" their talents, the radio allowed these performers to become professional musicians, traveling the state to play in one-room school houses, churches, and other local venues.

Some of the most popular North Carolina musicians were brother duets, such as Wiley and Zeke Morris, Jack and Curly Shelton, and Wade and Jack Mainer. These groups and many others blended their strong instrumental ability with harmony singing.

Later, Bill and Charlie Monroe would establish a style—tight vocals sung at lightning speed, accompanied by spell-binding instrumentals—that came to be known as Bluegrass music.

The music here remained a rich tradition. Some of the country's best and most beloved musicians hail for the Old North State.

CLAY AIKEN

The phenomenal popularity of the television show *American Idol* has shocked the world. We can't seem to get enough of watching completely untalented people humiliate themselves on national TV. We also seem to enjoy watching those who are truly talented develop those talents before our eyes and go on to realize their dreams of becoming THE American Idol.

One aspect of the show that seems to surprise the rest of the world but is nothing new to those of use living in the land of Magnolias and humidity is the number of Southern contestants. In fact, for four straight seasons, *Idol* was won by a Southerner and on more than one occasion, the second runner up and the winner was a Southerner. Really, with such a rich musical heritage, how could it be otherwise?

When Raleigh-native Clay Aiken (known as Clayton Grissom until he took his mother's maiden name) competed in the second *American Idol*, he came in second to Birmingham, Alabama-born Ruben Studdard.

When he first appeared before the *Idol* judges, Aiken's nerdy look had the judges convinced he'd be just another embarrassment. His voice, however, shocked the judges and the viewers and he was sent to Hollywood for the competition. He was cut his first round, but was brought back as a wild card. After that, he remained among the top contenders and, in fact, many believe that the network's call-in voting system was overwhelmed, allowing Studdard to be erroneously awarded top honors.

Aiken's loss was inconsequential, however, for he has become the most successful runner up. His first single went platinum within a month of its release. It was the fastest selling single in 2003. His first CD, *Measure of a Man*, debuted at Number One on the Billboard 200 and was the fastest selling CD in ten years.

In 2003, Aiken won the Fan's Choice Award and the American Music Awards, and his CD single won the Billboard award for the Best-selling Single of 2003.

FANTASIA BARRINO

Fantasia, as she is now billed, is another American Idol, only she actually won the title—and the highest accolades ever from the judges. Hers is a hard times story with a happy ending—well, at least a happy middle.

Born in High Point, she was sexually assaulted in high school, an experience that caused her to drop out. As a member of the Barrino family, she traveled the Carolinas and throughout the South performing. During that time, she gave birth to a daughter and became a struggling single mom.

In her audition for season three of *American Idol*, she blew away the judges and America with a stylized, gospel-influenced version of "Proud Mary." As soon as she opened her mouth, there was no doubt that she'd be "going to Hollywood."

Her rise to the top two on the show was rift with controversies, including an accusation of racism from Elton John, when she and two other talented African-Americans landed in the bottom three of one week's voting. There also was controversy over her status as a single mother and the idea that she would make a poor role model.

Fantasia just kept blowing away the competition with her performances, the best of which was her rendition of George Gershwin's "Summertime." That performance left her in tears from "feeling the song," and garnered the highest praise from the judges, with Randy Jackson naming it as the best performance ever from an *American Idol* contestant. The performance won an Emmy Award Nomination in 2004 for "The Greatest Television Moment." When she again sang the song in the final week of the contest, acerbic judge Simon Cowell declared her the best contestant among all the national and international champions since the show's inception. She won the competition in the highest finale vote in the show's history.

Since her win, Fantasia has racked up awards and hit records. Her first single entered the Billboard Hot 100 at number one, the first artist to do so with a first record. It stayed in that spot for eleven weeks, the longest consecutive stay for an American Idol, and was named the top selling single in 2004. Her CD was even more successful. In R&B radio, she was the first artist of any kind to have two of the top three songs. One of those songs, "Truth Is," set a record by staying in the number one spot for fourteen consecutive weeks.

Fanstasia has also appeared on television and won numerous awards and award nominations, including four Grammy Award nominations. And she has written a book, sort of. She dictated her story to a freelance writer, who put it all down for her. The reason she didn't write it herself is revealed in the book titled, *Life Is Not a Fairytale*. Remember? She dropped out of school early. The book reveals that she is functionally illiterate, a subject she also discussed on the television show, 20/20. She told the interviewer she is unable to read any of the contracts she has signed and learns the songs she performed by memorizing them.

There's more happy news there as well. She is being taught to read by tutors so that she can read to her daughter—and read those all important contracts. Maybe someday she will be able to look at a happy ending and revise her memoir to say, Life Is, Indeed, A Fairytale.

JOHN COLTRANE

John "Trane" Coltrane is considered the second—after Charlie Parker—most revolutionary and most imitated jazz saxophonist. Reared in High Point, he learned to play E-flat alto horn, clarinet, and saxophone around the age of fifteen. He enrolled at the Ornstein School of Music in Philadelphia, but a stint in the Navy in 1945 interrupted his studies.

Upon his return to the states, he began playing in jazz bands, where he switched back and forth from alto sax to tenor sax. He didn't become well known until 1955, when he joined a quintet led by Miles Davis. Throughout the fifties, an addiction to heroin and alcohol

John Coltrane is one of the most revolutionary and most imitated Jazz saxophonists.
Courtesy of the Coltrane family.

disrupted his career. When Davis fired him from his group because the addiction was affecting his performances, Coltrane vowed to kick the habit.

He returned to his home in Philadelphia and ordered his mother and his wife to lock him in his bedroom and feed him only bread and water. During this time, he underwent a religious epiphany, where he said he experienced God and made a deal with him. Asking God to free him from his addiction, he promised in return to make people happy with his music. God did and Trane, too, kept his end of the bargain, becoming so focused on his music that Davis remarked even a naked woman on stage could not distract him.

After his return, Coltrane joined Thelonius Monk, known as the High Priest of Bop. It was during this short six months, that Trane began to develop a technique known as "Sheets of Sound" during his solos. Most soloists hit a playing intensity that signaled the peak of their solo, but in this technique, Coltrane would hit that intensity and you'd think he was hitting his peak. But then he would wave into even higher intensity and continue to grow the sound, hitting the listener with wave after wave—sheet after sheet—of sound.

In 1959, Coltrane rejoined Davis's group, but he didn't last long, one reason being his propensity for playing really long solos, something Davis resented. In 1960, Coltrane started his own group and began experimenting in radical musical styles. Now he could play solo as long as he wanted, sometimes reaching thirty minutes and, at one point, playing a two-hour solo.

He also became a mentor for many young avant garde musicians, giving them exposure and lending legitimacy to the Free Jazz movement, a jazz style that incorporates dissonant sounds and random notes. Coltrane became known as the father of this movement, but he died before the movement could be truly developed and many say the movement died with him.

Coltrane succumbed to liver cancer in 1967 at age forty. He died too young, but left behind a huge legacy.

Roberta Flack

Killing me softly with his song…Killing me softly with his soooong! Sorry. That was my favorite song for a long time. Anyway, Roberta Flack was born in Asheville, but was reared in Arlington, Virginia, where her earliest musical influence came from the church.

At age nine, she began taking piano lessons and discovered an interest in a wide range of music, from pop to R&B to jazz. Into her teens, she developed an interest in classical music. Her piano talents developed rapidly and by age thirteen, she had placed second in a statewide contest for African-American students.

Her scholastic excellence rivaled her musical talents, allowing her to regularly skip grades, so much so that one year she was held back to allow her physical and emotional development to catch up. At age fifteen, she enrolled in Howard College on a full music scholarship.

Upon graduating with a degree in music education, Roberta became the first African-American student teacher in an all-white school in Maryland. The death of her father caused her to abandon plans for graduate school and return to North Carolina, where she took a teaching position at a small school in Farmville, North Carolina.

After her lifetime of exposure to higher education and classical music, Farmville was quite a culture shock. She was teaching English and music and found herself frustrated at trying to teach basic grammar to high school students, many of whom were older than she. Flack taught there a year then moved to Washington, where she found the same frustration. "How could I teach them [students] the National Anthem when they can't even read it?"

At this same time, Flack's musical career was beginning to build a head of steam. As a piano player at Washington's popular Tivoli Club, she accompanied opera singers who strolled into the room and during intermission, she played and sang. Her fame as a singer and piano player began to grow and she played several D.C. nightclubs, where she often shared the mic with such celebrities as Burt Bacharach, Liberace, and Johnny Mathis.

Her popularity led to a recording contract with Atlantic Records and her first album, *First Take*, was released in 1969. The album included the song "The First Time Ever I Saw His Face," but the song didn't become a hit until 1972, when Clint Eastwood chose it to be played in his movie *Play Misty for Me*. It was released as a single and instantly became a number one hit.

A few weeks later Flack's duo with Donnie Hathaway, "Where is the Love," was released as a single and in that year's

Grammy Awards, "The First Time…" won Record of the Year and Song of the Year and "Where is the Love" won Best Pop Vocal by a Duo. Ah, but Flack was just getting started.

Almost simultaneously her current single "Killing Me Softly," had hit gold sales status and was number one on both the pop and R&B charts. The album of the same name hit gold in two weeks and remained a top seller on all charts except country for months. In the 1974 Grammy Awards, the single won Record of the Year, Song of the Year, and Best Pop Vocal by a Female.

Though this phenomenal recording popularity lasted only through the seventies, Flack is still an immensely popular entertainer and she continues to record and to tour nationally and internationally. She is celebrated by VH-1 in its show *The 100 Greatest Women of Rock & Roll*, right alongside greats Tina Turner and Aretha Franklin. Some of today's hottest new talents, such as Alicia Keyes and Angie Stone cite her as an important influence on their music.

EARL SCRUGGS

Earl Scruggs was born to music. From his earliest days in Flint Hill, he was surrounded by the music played by his musical family. Daddy played fiddle and banjo, mama played the organ, and brothers and sisters joined right in there with their banjos and guitars. Scruggs said no other family could've loved music as much as they did.

Banjo pickers in Flint Hill preferred finger pickin' to the brushing or frailing styles favored by players further west—

oh, say, Blue Ridge. Scruggs agreed, but he put a twist to it. At age ten, after a fight with his brother, he stormed into his bedroom and began furiously picking on his banjo. He soon noticed that he was using a three-finger pickin' method as opposed to the usual two-finger method. The method worked well for him, winning him many blue ribbons in local fiddler conventions and a spot on local radio stations by the time he was a teenager.

After World War II, Scruggs quit his day job to pursue music as a career. In Nashville, he joined Bill Monroe's Blue Grass Boys and became one of the main influences on the development of Bluegrass music.

Another significant move came in 1948, when he left the Blue Grass Boys and teamed with guitarist Lester Flatt to form the Foggy Mountain Boys. The group was immensely popular and they played on radio stations across the South.

They became even more well-known when the group was chosen to sing and play the theme song of the immensely popular television series *The Beverly Hillbillies* in the sixties and also played in the movie *Bonnie and Clyde*. These events introduced traditional pickin' music into pop culture and suddenly a whole generation was enamored with blue grass music. Inspired by Scruggs's intense banjo playing, young citified musicians began learning to play.

In 1969, Scruggs left the Foggy Mountain Boys to play with his sons in the *Earl Scruggs Revue*, which blended bluegrass, folk, country, and rock music. The band was popular with audiences on college campuses, particular those in North Carolina.

In early 2000, Scruggs released his first album in seventeen years. Titled *Earl Scruggs and Friends*, the album takes Scruggs's traditional music and applies it to some of today's most popular performers and artists. It includes some pretty unlikely pairings—such as Elton John, Sting, and Melissa Etheridge. It also includes a few that make perfect sense—Johnny Cash, Rosanne Cash, John Fogarty, Don Henley, and Travis Tritt.

Scruggs's accolades include induction into the Country Music Hall of Fame, the North Carolina Music and Entertainment Hall of Fame, the International Bluegrass Association's Hall of Honor. He also received the National Medal of Arts, a star on Hollywood's Walk of Fame, and the 2002 Orville H. Gibson Lifetime Achievement Award— among others.

At age eighty-two, Scruggs is still touring, playing his music all over the country. In all his travels, however, he's never forgotten where he came from. "My music came up from the soil of North Carolina and I have been blessed that people in all parts of the world enjoy it," he says.

JAMES TAYLOR

"In my mind I'm going to Carolina…Can't you just see the sunshine…Can't you just feel the moonshine…" Ever wonder why James Taylor is daydreamin' about Carolina? Well, get a clue, man! Sweet Baby James grew up in Chapel Hill.

Taylor attributes much of his creative work to the influence of growing up in Carolina. It's the landscape, he's said that he remembers most. At the time he was growing up—in the fifties—the Morgan Creek area, where his family lived was mostly wooded and overgrown. It was a time before homes had a television in every room—in fact most didn't have a TV in any room. That left Taylor with lots of time on his hands, time to wander the woods and reflect, time to develop an imagination. He considers this time important to the development of his creative life.

And, of course, Carolina figures in his songs. "Carolina On My Mind" appeared on his first album, though it didn't become a hit until later. He also immortalized the Morgan Creek area in his song "Copperline," which appeared on the 1990s album *New Moon Shine*.

Taylor grew up in wealth and privilege, wintering in the family's eleven-room Chapel Hill home and summering in Martha's Vineyard. Despite his privileged childhood (or perhaps because of it) Taylor experienced depression so severe that at age seventeen, he had himself committed to a mental institution, a move he says saved his life. It wasn't his only experience with institutionalization. He was hospitalized at least once more in his early adulthood to break his addiction to heroin.

As a teenager, Taylor, who had taken up the guitar at a young age, had formed a band with a friend and even had released a record, which flopped. His break came after his hospitalization, when he moved to London and met Peter Asher, the manager of the Beatles. Paul McCartney was impressed with Taylor's music and encouraged Asher to represent the young singer. Taylor's first album, *James Taylor*, was released in 1968, but despite the participation of Paul McCartney and George Harrison on one track, the album was not successful.

After a second hospitalization in 1969, he released *Sweet Baby James*, which became a huge success, sparked mostly by the song "Fire and Ice," which is about Taylor's stint in the asylum and a friend who committed suicide. The popularity of *Sweet Baby James* sparked renewed interest in this first album. This is when "Carolina on My Mind" became a hit.

Taylor's sensitive and gentle acoustic songs helped to usher in a wave of singer/songwriters, including John Denver, Carole King, Joni Mitchell, Jackson Browne, and Carly Simon, whom Taylor married in 1972. His popularity became phenomenal throughout the seventies, with songs such as "You've Got a Friend," for which he won a Grammy; "Handy Man," for which he was awarded a Grammy for Best Male Pop Vocal Performance; and "How Sweet It Is (To Be Loved By You).

His popularity as a live performer and his refusal to cut back on touring led to a much-publicized divorce in 1983 from Simon, with whom he had two children. Although he no longer enjoys the phenomenal fame of the seventies, he has continued to record and tour, turning out award-winning music for more then thirty-five years.

Chapel Hill hasn't forgotten that it's got a friend in Sweet Baby James. In 2003, the bridge across Morgan Creek was renamed the James Taylor Bridge and the Chapel Hill Museum opened a permanent James Taylor exhibition, which includes memorabilia from Taylor's life. The exhibition includes photographs of Taylor when he was growing up in Chapel Hill, songbooks, various awards, and even a seventh-grade report card. Also included in the exhibit is the James Taylor Documentary Theater, a video media center featuring interviews and performances by Taylor.

Writers

No doubt about it, North Carolina is a hotbed of literary talent. We've got a whole host of critically-acclaimed and reader-beloved writers and journalists. Not only that. They all enjoy a singular honor: They've been deemed worthy of our Strange But True North Carolina tour!

Maya Angelou

Maya Angelou, one of the world's most critically-acclaimed and best-loved poets and authors, became a North Carolinian late. By the time she came to Winston-Salem in 1981, she had lived a full and exciting life in many incarnations. In her early twenties, she was a Creole cook, a streetcar conductor, an unwed mother, a madam, and a dancer. In later decades she became the editor of an English-language magazine in Egypt, a singer, an actress, a world traveler, an important civil rights activist, a lecturer, and the author of five collections of poetry and five autobiographies.

Her move to North Carolina added one more title to her resume: college professor. She came to accept a lifetime position as the first Reynolds Professor of American Studies at Wake Forest University—a position she still holds.

Of all these various and diverse professions, "writer" is how she says she describes herself. "And even to God," she says. "If I think he's forgotten my name, I'll ask him 'Remember me—the writer. The tall, black American lady, the Writer?'"

Hailed as one of the great voices of contemporary black literature, Angelou is a Renaissance woman who still travels the world sharing her legendary wisdom. Though she may describe herself as a writer, teaching is a profession to which she also is well suited. Her writings, which combine spirituality with a worldly earthiness, have touched and inspired millions—of all races.

She has written frankly of her painful childhood, being shuffled between her devout grandmother in Arkansas and her sophisticated mother in St. Louis. Her first book, *I Know Why The Caged Bird Sings*, speaks of those days and describes the rape at age seven that rendered her mute for five years. The five-year silence helped to find the unique voice of the poet she was to become.

Her advice to young poets and writers is to read out loud to hear how the language sounds in the mouth and the ear. Writing, and poetry especially, she says, is music for the human voice.

CLYDE EDGERTON

"Eudora Welty meets Mark Twain." That's how the *New York Times* describes Clyde Edgerton's writing. In this Durham native's books, many of which are set in the fictional town of

Listre, North Carolina, Edgerton uses satire, humor, and a cast of zany characters to deliver stinging criticisms of the Southern folkways and beliefs. These criticisms stirred much controversy and, indeed, his criticism of the Baptist religion in his first book, *Raney*, cost Edgerton his position as a faculty member at Campbell University, a Christian college in Buies Creek.

Despite his penchant for poking fun and stirring folks up, Edgerton is a popular writer, and his books are usually bestsellers. They also have received much critical acclaim and have garnered their author numerous literary awards. His book *The Floatplane Diaries* is hailed as an American classic. In addition, he has received five Notable Book Awards from the *New York Times*, a Guggenheim Fellowship, a Lyndhurst Fellowship, a North Carolina Award for Literature, and membership in the Fellowship of Southern Writers.

WILLIAM SYDNEY PORTER

This guy's a very famous writer. Never heard of him? Bet you have, you just don't know it. William Porter is better known by his pen name O.Henry. Aha!

Porter was born in 1862 on Polecat Creek in Guilford County and was raised in Greensboro by a spinster aunt. He lived in North Carolina until the age of nineteen, when he moved to Texas, where he held a variety of jobs, including that of a paying and receiving teller at the First National Bank of Austin. There, he seems to have developed a case of sticky fingers.

Convicted of embezzlement of bank funds, he was sentenced to five years in the Ohio Penitentiary, where he worked as the prison's night druggist. With a bit of time on his hands, Porter began writing, publishing his first short story from there under a pen name. He used several different pen names, but upon his early release for good behavior, he settled on O. Henry.

Moving to New York City, he soon became the most popular short story writer of his time. Showing their author's affection for human foibles, O.Henry's stories follow a formula

William Sydney Porter wrote under the name O. Henry.
Courtesy of Wikipedia.org.

dealing with ordinary people in ordinary situations and arriving at a surprise ending through some type of coincidence. His best known story is perhaps the "Gift of the Magi," a Christmas story involving a married couple strapped for money to buy gifts. They each sold their most prized possessions—she her long beautiful hair and he his gold watch—to buy the other a gift. From him, she received an expensive set of hair combs and from her, he received a watch fob. Surprise!

In 1907, Porter married his childhood sweetheart, Sarah Coleman of Weaverville. Happiness was short-lived, however, for he died in 1910. He's buried in Riverside Cemetery in Asheville.

THOMAS WOLFE

North Carolina's greatest contribution to American literature, Thomas Wolfe followed a writer's best course of action: write what you know. Unfortunately, what he knew was some pretty unflattering truths about some folks in his hometown of Asheville. Many of those folks never forgave him for the accurately drawn portrayals of them in his novels and short stories.

Wolfe first began as a playwright, but after numerous rejections, came to the conclusion that his work was better suited to the page rather than the stage. Although he wrote only four novels in his lifetime, they were long novels, filled with rhapsodic autobiographical prose. His first book, *Look Homeward Angel*, published in 1929, was dedicated to Alice Bernstein, a woman twenty years older with whom he had a turbulent affair. After publication of this book, Wolfe received a Guggenheim Fellowship, and using it as an excuse to travel to Europe, ended the affair.

Wolfe's second novel, *Of Time and River, A Legend Of A Man's Hunger In His Youth*, was published in 1935, followed by a collection of short stories. In 1937, Wolfe contracted pneumonia while traveling out West. Complications caused him to be hospitalized at Johns Hopkins Hospital, where surgery revealed the entire right side of his brain engulfed with tuberculosis. He died three days later on September 15, 1938, just short of his thirty-eighth birthday. He left behind a massive manuscript that eventually became his last two novels, *The Web and the Rock* and *You Can't Go Home Again*.

Strange But True Culture

Wolfe is buried in Asheville's Riverside Cemetery. His childhood home is now a memorial to him and is designated as a National Historic Landmark.